Developing Creative Thinking Skills

Based on over 15 years of groundbreaking research, *Developing Creative Thinking Skills* helps learners demonstrably increase their own creative thinking skills. Focusing on divergent thinking, 12 inventive chapters build one's capacity to generate a wide range of ideas, both as an individual and as a collaborator. This innovative textbook outlines a semester-long structure for the development of creative thinking skills and can easily be utilized as a self-directed format for those learning outside of a classroom. Readers are stimulated to maximize their own creativity through active exercises, challenges to personal limits and assumptions, and ideas that can help create powerful habits of variance.

Brad Hokanson is the Mertie W. Buckman Professor of Design Education at the University of Minnesota, USA. He has received multiple teaching awards and has a diverse academic record, including degrees in Art, Architecture, and Urban Design, and a Ph.D. in Instructional Technology.

Developing Creative Thinking Skills

An Introduction for Learners

Brad Hokanson

Routledge
Taylor & Francis Group

NEW YORK AND LONDON

First published 2018
by Routledge
711 Third Avenue, New York, NY 10017

and by Routledge
2 Park Square, Milton Park, Abingdon, Oxon, OX14 4RN

Routledge is an imprint of the Taylor & Francis Group, an informa business

© 2018 Taylor & Francis

Library of Congress Cataloging-in-Publication Data
A catalog record for this book has been requested

ISBN: 978-1-138-93955-4 (hbk)
ISBN: 978-1-138-93956-1 (pbk)
ISBN: 978-1-315-67487-2 (ebk)

Typeset in Optima
by Apex CoVantage, LLC

Contents

Acknowledgments

I would like to acknowledge those who have given me opportunities to develop the classes, ideas, and directions to encourage people to become more creative, and now to write this book.

I begin by thanking Gerry Allan for introducing me to the idea of creative problem solving, as well as my colleagues Kim Johnson and Becky Yust at the University of Minnesota, who have supported my teaching and research efforts. They saw the vision of a class on creativity and helped it develop to become an important part of the curriculum. I also owe a debt to my students, who have helped me better understand creativity and learning and who have provided countless moments of joy in their own creative work.

I am grateful to Alex Masulis for his support in developing this book and to the great staff at Taylor & Francis for their help, wisdom, and direction. Most substantially, I'd like to thank my wife Betsy Henderson, who helped make this book possible with her support and optimism.

1 An Introductory Story

Imagination is more important than knowledge. For while knowledge defines all we currently know and understand, imagination points to all we might yet discover and create.
—Albert Einstein

One weekend years ago, I rode my bicycle 12 miles over to where I was working. My parents and friends were out of town, and I was using the time get a little more work done. On the way home, I had a flat in my rear tire down the street from a drug store. I didn't have a patching kit to fix it, and neither did the gas station on the corner. I remember thinking that I needed to be very inventive or I would have an extremely long walk home with my forlorn bicycle.

The image of that long, long walk home may have motivated me to come up with a creative solution, so I went into the drug store and started scanning the shelves for something that would spark an idea. In the school supplies aisle I found rubber cement. In the party section I found balloons. Together these approximated the materials of a repair patch kit. It worked, and I walked the bike to the corner and filled the tire at the gas station's air hose, and then I rode home in good time.

I didn't anticipate the problem and didn't have a defined solution, a situation we all encounter frequently. But it's illustrative of the large and small changes we will need to address in our lives. Having the ability to develop many and different creative answers to the problems that inevitably pop up can save us from fates far worse than a long walk home.

Creativity will always be in demand because the future will always be different from the present in which we are comfortable. We will always be faced with problems and opportunities we couldn't anticipate. All of us hear of trends and changes that are occuring in the world. New technologies are being invented, the climate is changing, and social structures are evolving and in conflict. We will need to deal with these changes in our everyday lives, and in how we work, govern, and interact with other people. More "new" is coming, whether in cereal, cars, laws, ideas, or problems. The rules are going to change. We will need new habits of mind to meet these challenges.

What we know now will not be enough to address future changes and challenges. Knowledge is not static in any field, and anyway simply having knowledge is not enough, because knowledge must be synthesized, and challenged. How we will solve problems will involve a lot more than just having more information. We—you—will need to be creative. You will need to be creative in what information you use, find, combine, and manipulate; creative in what information you find and in what information you ignore; and creative in what tools, resources, and skills you apply to the problem. Finally, you will have to be creative in who you work with, who you don't work with, and in how you collaborate and work with others. While we are going to live and work in a knowledge economy, with information as its currency, shaping and directing the use of that currency depends on our own creativity.

In business, at work, in life, and as you enter the university, one skill will be the most important to your success: your ingenuity, which is your ability to be creative. Businesses around the world recognize this skill as important and seek out the most creative workers for their enterprises. A recent poll by IBM of over 1,500 business executives from around the world listed creativity as the most desirable competancy for leaders in business. Significantly, countries around the world have changed their school curricula to improve the creativity of their students. The United Kingdom, for example, has reorganized its secondary school curriculum to encourage the ability for students to develop new ideas (Cox, 2005). China is changing its educational direction to develop more than cognitive intelligence and to encourage more creativity as described in Zhao's *World Class Learners* (2012). Similar efforts are underway in Singapore, Korea, Taiwan, and Denmark. This is a need of national and world importance. In general, innovation and inventiveness build prosperity by developing new products, services, and processes. It is in a nation's interest to have a creative workforce.

Creativity is not limited to the arts. There is a difference between visual ability and creativity. Some exceptionally skilled painters may be proficient in representational art without being terribly creative. They're just painting what they see. And while many people claim they aren't creative because they can't draw, they may be exceptionally skilled at inventing solutions to challenging problems. We are all creative to some extent and can build on our current creative capability.

Like artistic skill, intelligence is often linked to creativity, but being smarter doesn't necessarily make you more creative. However, like intelligence, creativity can be improved through effort. Both are needed to be successful. Once you're at a certain level of intelligence, the difference in success can be ascribed to creativity. This is recognized through the achievements of a lifetime; research has shown that creativity is three times as strong an indicator of lifetime achievement as intelligence (Plucker, 1999).

Happily, your level of creativity is not fixed, and this book will help *you* enhance and extend your creativity. Creative problem solving can be developed and improved using a number of well-understood techniques and sources. This book presents some of those techniques through learning activities and challenges, projects, and quizzes.

Througout the book, you will be given a number of challenges that are designed to cultivate creative mental habits. You will do things you have never done before and things you have only wished you could do. The great value of this book is that the work is yours, and your work will be much of what is talked about in the book. While much of the book is focused on challenges and exercises, there will also be supporting informational material to help you better understand creativity. This book is founded on a rich body of knowledge on creativity that will support your developing practice. The idea here is of "doing" this book. It contains a lot of exercises and challenges designed to help you understand yourself and creativity. Finally, you can even use this book as an excuse when trying new things. When undertaking one of the exercises that follow, just say "it's for class," and most people will give you carte blanche. You'll engage other people in your school, family, or community, and you will hopefully have fun during the process. In the end, your creative thinking skills will have increased, and you'll also have a better understanding of creativity as a skill that can be learned and fostered.

It's time to talk about commitment. In order to get the most out of the material, you're going to need to consciously choose to be more creative. It will influence your life and those around you but will take some time and practice. In the end, you will be more creative.

Though you probably have a lot to do in your life in addition to this book and its activities, we know that mastery of any skill—whether it is tennis, French, or creativity—takes practice. Therefore, in order to get the best results from the book, it's important for you to make a commitment to becoming more creative. Good habits developed here will to improve your performance and integrate creativity into your already busy life.

First, I'd suggest that you set aside a specific time to complete the work from the book every week. This may be every Friday afternoon, every Saturday morning, or Monday in the middle of the night. Just keep that time consistent. That'll help you complete the work. The time is your choice, but building this habit will help you accomplish that much more.

I'd also recommend you work with a partner, a small group, or even a class. Having others to share your experiences with is a great learning experience, and there are exercises that require a partner to complete later in the book.

Make sure you check out the Textbox examples that support the development of your creativity, as well as the larger Do Something Different projects that you will see throughout the book.

Finally, I'd strongly recommend you use a journal to record your thoughts and to save your pictures of the things that you do. You'll be able to see your progress and be able to share your effort with others, and it's also a good way to record your ongoing ideas.

Now, let's get started!

How Creative Are You?

The quantity of civilization is measured by the quality of imagination.

—Victor Hugo

Testing Your Creativity

As with any learning activity, it can be helpful to know just how skilled you really are. There should be an honest evaluation of your capability for originality before you read any further. This will help you understand your current capabilities as well as those that can be developed during the course of reading this book. So, just like we weigh ourselves when we start a diet, we'll check our creativity before we begin.

In addition, trying these ways of assessing your creativity will also help you understand the nature of creativity itself. Not only can each test help you understand how creative you are, but it also will give you a better understanding of the phenomenon of creativity, and you'll know a little more how to improve yourself, as well.

There are a number of different ways to evaluate creativity, each looking at different aspects of creativity and variants of its definition. This chapter will describe some of these methods and give you the chance to test yourself to develop an understanding of how creative you, the reader, are. The next chapter will focus on many of the definitions of creativity and how it is recognized. Having a measure of your own creativity will also help you understand the ideas presented throughout the book.

One common way to evaluate creativity is through the creative accomplishments of your life: your creative production in generating new ideas, products, artifacts, or procedures. We could also look at really creative individuals and see their efforts. Some researchers find this to be most valid as it accurately measures performance in the real world, not just over the course of a small test on one day. However, measurements of creativity like this are historical; they look back at your life as opposed to being predictive, anticipating your future progress. And in the case of the famous creatives, they don't tell us about our own creativity.

Evaluating Yourself

We could, of course, just ask how you are. Chances are, if you say you are creative, likely you are a little more creative than people who say they're not. It also could be that those who claim to be creative are more willing to accept risks, try new things, and reach for different ideas—all components of being creative. You know your own habits. And saying you're creative might actually *be* an accurate evaluation of your capability. It might also reflect other people's opinions. If they think you are creative, there is a good chance that you are. It also means you have an open license to try new things, so it's a win-win. And the *correspondence principle* of psychology holds that thinking you are creative and seeking more creative activities will develop your creativity further.

However, having someone "self-report" their level of creativity might not be that accurate; it might be inflated by our own self-confidence or lessened by our mood, our context or our friends, or even our blood sugar. Few people would accept that judgment as being accurate. Using ways to objectively measure our creativity would help in providing an honest, accurate, outside evaluation of our creative skills (Roberts, 2004).

Let's begin by examining our own life of how creative we are, and the aspects of our life we could observe that would indicate our capacity for creative behavior. In this exercise is a series of questions; be honest in evaluating yourself as this will help you get an accurate understanding of how creative you are.

Creativity can also be examined by a number of objective and external ways, from looking at the long-term history of widely recognized creative people, to reviewing our long-term history, to reviewing our habits and daily actions, to checking how we perform when given specific challenges.

Exercise 2.1 Self-Report Exercise

Please circle the answer that best describes you and how you are creative.
Circle number: 1 Never 2 Not so much 3 Sometimes 4 Often 5 Most of the time

	Circle number				
	Almost never				**Most of the time**
1. I think logically to find an answer for problems	1	2	3	4	5
2. I'm good at combining different ideas	1	2	3	4	5
3. I can come up with solutions and ideas most people don't have	1	2	3	4	5
4. I often combine different ideas to solve problems	1	2	3	4	5
5. I am efficient in developing a workable idea	1	2	3	4	5
6. I can come up with more ideas than my friends	1	2	3	4	5
7. My ideas and answers have a lot of detail	1	2	3	4	5
8. Many of my ideas are unusual and eccentric	1	2	3	4	5
9. I'm willing to experiment and try out my ideas in public	1	2	3	4	5
10. I look for different ways to understand a problem	1	2	3	4	5
11. On complex problems, I carefully weigh my choice of a solution	1	2	3	4	5
12. People ask me for ideas when they're stumped	1	2	3	4	5
13. I like to share my solutions and ideas with others	1	2	3	4	5
14. I help other people improve and build on their ideas	1	2	3	4	5
15. I have a lot of different and unusual ideas	1	2	3	4	5
16. I usually find a larger theme in solving any challenge	1	2	3	4	5

Exercise 2.1 Continued

	Circle number				
	Almost never			Most of the time	
17. People seek me out for my unique ideas	1	2	3	4	5
18. People expect me to come up with unusual ideas	1	2	3	4	5
19. I see a number of different solutions in most problems	1	2	3	4	5
20. I work hard to find my best idea quickly as it's more effective	1	2	3	4	5
Total					

Our creativity can accurately be evaluated by giving challenges or prompts and getting responses. This is the most common creativity testing that is done.

Performance Challenges

These are performance challenges, similar to those developed by early creativity researchers. They are brief, reliable, and inexpensive, and they can help us better understand creativity in general and our skill level in particular. The tests included here are cost-free and can give us a good understanding of our creative capability. They can also serve as exercises to develop our skill.

The idea is to measure how good you are at quickly developing a wide range of different answers, how broadly ranging those answers are, how well you make unusual connections, and how the answers are of different types or concepts.

The idea is for creativity to be measured by having someone complete a series of tasks over a given period of time. A number of tests, requiring either written and drawn answers, were developed by Paul Torrance and J. P. Guilford in the 1950s, and hundreds of thousands of people have been tested using this method. These are timed, lasting from five minutes to 40 minutes, and they can be easily scored. Individuals taking the test can score their own creativity test results, but most tests are sent to a professional scoring service for accuracy and convenience. There are a wide range of other published tests for creativity.

Included in this chapter are a series of brief challenges that will help you rate your creativity. Each will take five or ten minutes and will give you a beginning understanding of your creative ability. They're all designed for self-grading, easy to score, and hopefully, interesting to complete. And by doing them, you'll be taking the first steps to increasing your own creativity.

Alternative Uses Test

There's a great quote from Linus Pauling, Nobel Laureate, who said, "The best way to have a good idea is to have a lot of ideas and then to throw the bad ones away." Having a lot of different ideas is a great way to be more creative, and the most frequently used test of creativity focuses on this skill, called *divergent thinking.*

The Alternative Uses Test measures your capability to develop a lot of ideas. This is one main component of creativity and probably the most central aspect of the skill.

This test names a common object and challenges you to develop as many possible alternative uses for the object. To do the test, you'll need a timer, something to write with, and paper to record your ideas. Come up with as many ideas as you can, using the entire time for the challenge. The more answers, the better, even if the ideas are unusual or weird. You should respond in the language with which you are most comfortable. This will allow you the greatest capability in generating new ideas. Using your best language is the most effective way to develop and present your creativity.

Write down as many different and unusual things can you do with a tin can. Use as many tin cans as you want, and they can be of any size large or small. Try to think about the most unusual and different uses you can imagine. There are no wrong answers. It's good to be different. Make sure you use a full five minutes. Write them down in Exercise 2.2. Start your timer, and you can begin!

Figure 2.1 Alternative Uses Test: Tin Can

Exercise 2.2: Alternative Uses Test

1. _____

2. _____

3. _____

4. _____

5. _____

6. _____

7. _____

8. _____

9. _____

10. _____

11. _____

12. _____

13. _____

14. _____

15. _____

How to Evaluate the Alternative Uses Test

The first step in any evaluation of the Alternative Uses Test is to eliminate the answers that don't deal with the question. While going outside the rules is often a good model of creative thought, in this case the idea must be a real response to the task at hand. (Creativity is something that is novel and appropriate [Sternberg & Lubart, 1999], not something that's completely different, thrown in there at random.) So, first, eliminate any answer that doesn't use at least one tin can in some way.

Now count the number of your answers that do something with a tin can. This count will give you what is called the *fluency*, a measurement of the divergent thinking ability. This measurement can be very accurate: Testing this ability repeated times, using repeated models, can provide an accurate understanding of the most common denominator of creativity. Should you wish to re-challenge yourself, you can also use other prompts, such as newspaper, cardboard, blankets, or paper clips.

How many answers should you develop? In general, people come up with more unusual answers the more total answers they develop. A good goal based on my beginning testing of my students would be 11–12 for a five-minute test and 24 for a ten-minute test. In general, people don't develop unusual answers or original answers until they give at least ten different answers. They go through the easy, common answers first, and often just stop at one.

Number of Tin Can Answers: _____

Of course, this only gives you a number of ideas that may seem like random words without meaning and without a value on the page. The next understandable aspect of creativity is called *originality*, and it measures how rare the answer is compared to what everyone else in society would give as answers.

Based on data gathered from my own online research sources, here are the top answers to the prompts of tin can: holder, container, instrument, music, cup, phone, pot, hat, food, toy, and vase. If you had answers other than these, great. If they all matched the list, you should get out more. Most would agree that rare or unique answers are ones that have a higher potential to indicate creativity (see, for example, Kudrowitz & Wallace, 2013).

Number of Original Answers: _____

Finally, one of the tougher parts of evaluation is figuring different types of answers. Most answers that deal with a tin can are mentally connected with some form of construction; you could do a wall, floor, fence, barbeque, or chimney; changing away from building or construction will force a different type of use. Consider using a tin can in the kitchen, bedroom, or classroom, and more divergent uses will occur. This component of creativity is called *flexibility* and is connected to more *transformative* change. For our evaluation, we should count the various different types of uses that are present in your answers.

Number of Different Types of Answers: _____

You can also do this test over but will need to use a different subject, so exchange "paper clip" for "tin can," and try it again. Again, use the timer, and record your results. This might be more than your first try or less; over time and with practice, you'll do better. You will be retested at the end of the book, looking for your progress.

Write down the number of ideas you had and the number of "original" answers you had that weren't on the list of common answers. It's good to be different.

Paper Clip Answers: _____ Number of Original
Answers: _____

The common answers are: hold/holder, chain, key, belt, draw, necklace, pick, ring, art, bracelet, card, earrings, and game.

Thinking of alternative uses for any everyday object is a simple but great task to continue to develop your creativity; it can be done anywhere with any type of object.

Different Consequences Challenge

We also need to test our imagination in addressing real-world problems. While developing alternative uses for everyday objects is simple to use, a lot of our challenges and problems in real life are more complex . . . and we do need to develop a wide range of answers and to build on our original ideas. The challenge has been made to have an unusual starting point to encourage more diverse thinking. Again, we'll set a timer for five minutes and write down answers to the situation.

Here's the challenge: Let's imagine you woke up one morning and found that your car, mobile phone, or personal computer was gone, maybe stolen or lost. What would be the *advantages* of this problem? What could be the positive consequences of this event? Write your choice of the above at the top of the list, then use the entire five minutes to generate as many positive outcomes for this event as possible; don't be afraid to include unusual answers as well. And don't limit the number of your answers; record as many possible answers as you can.

Exercise 2.3: Consequences Test

1. _____

2. _____

3. _____

4. _____

5. _____

6. _____

7. _____

8. _____

9. _____

10. _____

11. _____

12. _____

13. _____

14. _____

Ideas: _____ Added Details: _____

Once you've used the entire five minutes coming up with possible advantages to the situation, spend five more minutes and add details to each of your answers, on or below the same line. The more, the better. You might also find you have more starting answers as well. A detail would be a modification or extension of the initial idea, describing materials, process, people, or locations.

This will give an understanding of your skill for elaboration, one of the other ways that creativity is measured.

Again, count your initial answers; this is a measurement of your fluency. And then, separately, count the details that were added on each of your answers.

Ideas: _____ Number of Details: _____

It might be asked why this test is different from the previous tests? While it does some of the same things as the Tin Can / Alternative Uses Test, it also starts looking at your everyday creativity and ability to develop ideas in a real context. And to provide another way to evaluate creativity, it also looks at how ideas are developed and improved.

People frequently ask why the exercises are timed. Some people are slower to develop new ideas, and their ideas can be good. It's true that given unlimited time, most people could come up with a lot of answers. These measurements, however, are based on the ability to rapidly develop a lot of ideas as, in most cases, time is of the essence and new ideas need to be developed rapidly. Additionally, testing itself should not take a lot of time; it's better to get a reasonably accurate assessment of the ability to come up with ideas as opposed to trying to make sure you get every possible idea. In any case, using a single set time period provides a way to evaluate yourself now and later without involving you into some long drawn-out test.

One of the balances that needs to be included with any testing of creativity is the raw number of answers and the quality, or detail, of those answers. Both are valuable, with the number of answers (*fluency*) and the details added to the answers (*elaboration*) serving as slightly different ways to measure creativity.

If someone's ideas all take a long time to explain due to the detail of the idea, there will be fewer ideas in the first place, i.e., lower fluency. But at the same time, there will be a higher level of elaboration presented in the work. Creative people need to balance the number of ideas with the details included in each idea . . . which is why this test lets you develop a lot of ideas first, adding details later.

Remote Associates Test

Creativity develops in the brain through connections that are made between different brain cells holding different thoughts. We make new ideas out of our experiences and knowledge. This is called the Associative Theory. For example, my experience in traveling to Argentina will help me have ideas about the nature of dance, which might also influence my ideas about movement and fashion. That's one reason why some theories strongly emphasize the diversity of experience that one has in supporting creativity. One's brain has more unusual things to work with to make connections that form new ideas.

Since new ideas come mainly from re-connecting or combining old ideas and experiences, how well you make those combinations is another question. While a lot of different forms of experience may give you the raw material with which to generate new ideas, you might not be interested or able to make the connections. One way to test your connection capability is through the Remote Associates Test. It's fairly simple, you can score it yourself, and, like the Alternative Uses Test, it's fun to do.

As we've seen before, *originality*, an aspect of creativity, is one way to evaluate how creative something is. Creativity is the ability to generate ideas that are both novel (new in context) and appropriate (able to be used). And something that is novel is *original* if it is rare or new in context. And therefore, we're looking for things that are very different or *remote*. That's why this test is called the Remote Associates Test; it's looking for connections or associations and seeking those connections that are often unusual or rare.

So here we'll try the Remote Associates Test. Each item has three starting words to be linked in some way with a fourth. The fourth word can be added at the beginning or end of each word. Time your effort on the test, and stop working after ten minutes. You'll also complete the test at the end of the book. Here's an example of some word sets:

Starting Words	Corresponding Word
show • life • row	boat
night • wrist • stop	watch
duck • fold • dollar	bill
rocking • wheel • high	chair

Now try to solve these as practice; add a fourth word in the set that connects with the other three words.

Starting Words	Corresponding Word
dew • comb • bee	_____
fountain • baking • pop	_____
preserve • ranger • tropical	_____
aid • rubber • wagon	_____

Practice Answers

The correct answers are honey, soda, forest, and band. If you had other answers that fit as well as these do, that's even better.

There are 15 elements of varying difficulty. A comparable test will occur at the end of the book. To keep this a reasonable challenge, stop and just record your score after ten minutes. If you complete all the word cues in less than ten minutes, record that time. Don't, however, work longer than ten minutes unless you like the challenge.

Exercise 2.4: Remote Associates Test

Find a fourth word that fits with the other three in some way, on the front or the back; complete as many as you can in ten minutes. If you finish sooner, write down your time. If you get stuck for more than 15 seconds or so, go to the next one, and come back when you've finished the rest.

flake • mobile • cone   _____

safety • cushion • point   _____

dream • break • light   _____

political • surprise • line   _____

high • district • house   _____

worm • shelf • end   _____

flower • friend • scout   _____

print • berry • bird   _____

date • alley • fold   _____

cadet • capsule • ship   _____

stick • maker • point   _____

fox • man • peep   _____

dust • cereal • fish   _____

food • forward • break   _____

peach • arm • tar   _____

palm • shoe • house   _____

wheel • hand • shopping   _____

home • sea • bed   _____

sandwich • house • golf   _____

boot • summer • ground   _____

Please Record Your Time: _____ Number Completed: _____

Answers Evaluation of Remote Associates Test

The word combinations themselves vary in difficulty based on our ordinary use of language. The capability to answer this test will also vary with language ability. People who take the test who are not native English speakers may not score as well as someone who is highly fluent. This is because stored ideas and thoughts are often symbolized through spoken words as well as the fact this test works specifically with language.

While the answers below provide an answer, there may be other words that complete the group in ways that are unique to your context; for example, the triad "high • district • house" can be completed by the words "school" or "court."

Remote Associates Test Answers

flake • mobile • cone	snow
safety • cushion • point	pin
dream • break • light	day
political • surprise • line	party
high • district • house	school or court
worm • shelf • end	book
flower • friend • scout	girl
print • berry • bird	blue
date • alley • fold	blind
cadet • capsule • ship	space
stick • maker • point	match
fox • man • peep	hole
dust • cereal • fish	bowl
food • forward • break	fast
peach • arm • tar	pit
palm • shoe • house	tree
wheel • hand • shopping	cart
home • sea • bed	sick
sandwich • house • golf	club
sage • paint • hair	brush
boot • summer • ground	camp

Conclusion

Do these challenges help you figure out a better answer for some problem? Not directly. Note that the main purpose of the book is to help people develop a more divergent set of answers or ideas, from which to choose more appropriate, or at least different, responses. In general, people tend to be "solution focused" in settling into the first answer they can find that is satisfactory. Further answers may appear to be less valuable and/or at least different, breaking new ground away from the tried and true.

Creativity implies that the answer will be different and that, in many cases, the given answer will be unusual and not immediately acceptable.

Completing these simple tests is not just about developing a clear understanding of your current state of creativity. It can also be a beginning for development of your own creative skills; you've seen how it can be evaluated; responding to those questions and challenges—by practicing, doing, and integrating this stuff into your life—will make you more creative.

Now you have some understanding of how creativity is measured, and you have a better understanding of your own creativity. In this writing, we'll build on that understanding to help you develop your own creativity. And, at the end of the book, we'll see how much you've changed through the course of this book.

3 | **Methods of the Book**

Creative thinking is not a talent; it is a skill that can be learnt. It empowers people by adding strength to their natural abilities which improves teamwork, productivity and where appropriate, profits.

—Edward de Bono

Beliefs, Habits, Skills, and Knowledge

The skills of creativity can be applied to many forms of learning and knowledge; they are not just for the arts and design fields. For example, an engineer will know how to solve problems in one way, but developing multiple ideas that may not be as initially apparent can lead to breakthroughs. This book will introduce some methods of triggering more ideas. These methods will help you to generate more ideas, and, by following these processes, you can increase your innate creativity.

We'll also examine some of the research-based knowledge about creativity. There is a rich body of knowledge on creativity that will support your creative practice, and much of this book is founded on that research. Some key findings include the high value of creativity in terms of lifetime achievement, the ability to develop one's creative skill, and the value of habits and practice (Plucker, 1999; Scott, et al., 2004; Bronson & Merryman, 2010; Cox, 2005).

However, in the end, you will need to forge your own path, evaluate your ideas, and engage with others to build new ideas. While learning about some methods and tricks for making ourselves more creative, we're going to do small exercises to increase our capability as well as larger challenges to stretch our skill.

The structure of this book is based on four levels of learning and involvement: beliefs, habits, skills, and knowledge. Knowledge, the traditional lead component of most academic courses, is the least important aspect of the effort. Beliefs, habits, and skills are all more important. This is about a change in you, the reader.

Beliefs come from one's own experience with and exposure to ideas about creativity. Perhaps the most important component of being creative is a belief in one's own creative capability. We must recognize that creativity is present in us all and that the level of creativity of anybody can be increased if they choose to do so. You should believe in your own creativity and also act in ways that encourage you to develop your creativity. Having habits that help you develop and build your own creative skills are essential.

Habits can be described as ways in which we do the same things, but they also can be characteristics that regularly develop, demonstrate, and increase creativity. These types of routines are important in welcoming and seeking new ideas and divergent thoughts. These creative habits include the consistent development of divergent ideas, regularly providing more responses than are required, involving oneself in challenging and different activities, and consistently seeking to be more creative.

The skills of creativity need development as well—whether in the process of making something habitual or in the conscious use of a creative methodology. Practice in the techniques will make them more habitual, even in the simplest task of generating more ideas. At first, there are personal limits as to how well multiple concepts or ideas can be developed. The ability to create more will come through practice—a practice that must be internalized and be part of your everyday experience.

Understanding the Theory

One thing that is valuable in learning anything is to understand the methods of learning and what is being used to help you learn. This goes for creativity as well.

So how does one get to be creative? Are you just born that way? Or not born that way? Is creativity tied to how intelligent you are? Can you change how creative or how intelligent you are?

This book is focused not on learning information but rather on developing creative skills. This means the emphasis is not on information delivery but rather on actively learning and doing creative exercises.

First of all, our creativity is, in some part, based on our native intelligence. As with intelligence, we can change and improve what we naturally have. We can learn through schooling and through experience, and become smarter. Research has proved that we can also develop our creativity through training and effort, just as we can develop our own intelligence (Scott, et al., 2004).

Creativity is a trait of your personality and can be focused and improved through work and effort. Luckily for all of us, the development of creativity, the actual process, is fun and enjoyable, and it can be done anywhere. At the same time, you can think of this process as your creativity workout space. One way to think about developing your creativity is like physical exercise, like building muscles in a gym. If we use our creativity, we'll get stronger creativity "muscles"; if we don't use it, we'll get flabby and fall back on our old habits.

How the Book Works

Specifically, how do you improve your own creativity, and how will this be presented in this book? Well, the best way to have people learn something is to have them actively work on what they need to learn. In other words, rather than simply reading about something, you need to do something that applies what you are learning and developing. In order to become more creative, you need to consciously do things that will make you more creative. So this book is about doing stuff, and it isn't going to only be about presenting information and talking about very creative people that aren't you. It's about *you* becoming more creative.

This is a very serious pursuit. We know a lot of what is done in education today focuses on spreading and remembering information. Teachers present information, and students are expected to remember that same information. The development of new ideas, new combinations, or new understanding is generally not addressed in the educational process. While creativity does break through at times, this structure is effective at limiting creativity by focusing on information rather than developing new ways to use that same information (Bronson & Merryman, 2010).

While the learning effort for creativity is a fun process, it remains a serious need for society, as it is where new inventions, new ideas, and new solutions will begin. It's fun, but it's the most important thing I do, developing the creative ability of others.

Your success will be in part determined by your active involvement with the challenge as well as your representation of that engagement though writing and visual means. Significant parts of your success are also how much change occurs in your life and how public the action is. Eating a food from a different ethnic group may be different from your life experience, but it may not represent a significant challenge or unusual event for the majority of society; as a practice, however, it can lead to developing your own divergent thinking. That divergent thinking can be applied in any field of work or study.

One of the more important concepts of the book (and of my classes) is that the only wrong answer is one single answer. While most fields hold that there is a unique, correct answer to any given problem, within creativity (and other subjective areas) there are only good, better, and worse answers. The world is more complex than one answer, and, in reaching for other possible answers, we will, in theory, find Einstein's relatives. All of these divergent answers need to be examined at the beginning of solving any problem. Here, the number of correct answers is not "one."

Logically, for every exercise and challenge in this book, you must look for more answers, only later to select and improve what could be the best answer.

Generating More Ideas

Two essential aspects of creativity are often lumped together as part of "finding a good idea." We need to distinguish between the two. These are the accepted essential aspects of creativity: *divergent* thinking (coming up with ideas) and *convergent* thinking (picking the best idea to advance). Both are needed for the exercise of creativity, and each must be understood.

Convergent thinking deals with selecting and developing ideas. It's based on logic, judgment, and your own knowledge, and it is often related to specific expertise. Divergent thinking, however, is more universal and is the ability to develop a large number of multiple ideas. Divergent thinking is the focus of this book, and the efforts here can be applied to any field from poetry to farming to sales. There will be more about divergent and convergent thinking in the next chapter.

The most effective way to become more creative is to develop more ideas. While we often want *better* finished ideas, becoming more creative first means having more ideas with which to work.

Ideas are cheap and at the same time valuable. With some practice, we can come up with many different ideas in our mind, and those different ideas can have substantial value. Ideas, like digital images, cost very little to invent. We create them in our minds out of our experiences and knowledge. We don't have to pay for each idea that we create. Having more ideas will also increase the possibility of having more *good* ideas. And since we can make ideas for free, we might as well make a lot of them, and have fun doing it.

The Habit of Variance (Varying)

Generating a lot of ideas all the time is a good habit, but it's not the sole habit we need to be more creative. We need to find new things, find new ideas, meet new people, and encounter new challenges on an ongoing basis. While we need to break out of habits that have us do the same old thing, we also need to develop a brand new habit, one where the actual habit is to continue to do new and different things.

This is a challenging idea, because we've all spent much of our lives seeking to get good habits like brushing our teeth, eating a healthy diet, and exercising. Similarly, our decisions and thoughts have been organized into habits about work patterns, political beliefs, and entertainment. We've limited the cognitive effort, shortcutting our mental exertion by doing the same things. Now the habit we need to pursue and develop is the habit to vary. You need to consciously change what you are doing, experimenting, and exploring, by being different throughout your entire life.

For example, you could start wearing different-colored socks on each foot . . . and that would get to be a habit in itself. You could order different food next time you go to your favorite restaurant, or drive a different way home tomorrow from work, school, or the market. Each of these simple changes will begin to add up, bringing in new information. This provides you with more mental elements from which to develop new ideas. You might find your socks more interesting, you might find a great new dish at the restaurant, or you might find a small park just off your regular route home. What else could you see? Your general goal is to consistently do something different.

Effort

One thing I understand from developing creativity for multiple years is the need to continue the effort for a substantial period of time and to dedicate yourself to this pursuit of creativity. Just like learning a musical instrument, or French, or tennis, it does take a substantial and conscious effort to develop one's own creativity. If you really want to change, it will take a sustained effort over an extended period of time.

Most skills require a complex set of skills. Expertise or mastery is slow to develop and often takes years of attention and effort. Creativity is like this, but it is not limited to any single domain, and it can be extended across your whole life regardless of what you do for work or pleasure.

Gaining Permission

Experience has also taught me that it will take a couple of weeks to get used to the activities: to acting strange in public and even among your family. Not to worry. The people in your life will eventually find your efforts acceptable. You can recognize how creative you were in the beginning through the tests and through your own experience, and you can observe your own changes by your ability to go further and to be less afraid of challenge. Over the years, my students have said completing the "differents" encouraged them to do much more in their lives than they ever imagined.

A lot of times, people step back from what is possible and creative because of their own personal limitations. They don't want to be perceived as different, unusual, or weird, and therefore they sacrifice their own creativity to this form of shyness. The pressure to conform, to go along with a social group, or to be the same as one's peers is very strong, and it does not help in advancing new ideas. Inherently, to be creative means that others may find the ideas presented strange, out of place, or even just different, which is one of the necessary ingredients of any creative idea.

As I have said, our creative efforts are often constrained by our own personal limitations. We edit our own ideas and limit our own actions. We don't believe we are creative or that our work has merit. I see this in class. Students don't want to appear silly or stupid and do not act on good ideas or good questions. They're afraid of doing something out of the ordinary or different, and they settle for a much less interesting idea.

In doing a number of things that are, by definition, different, we are building up a callous on our shyness, and on our tendency to be embarrassed in public when we are acting different from most other people. Most times, the things you do in the pursuit of creativity won't be viewed as that weird or offbeat (although some might be if you are lucky!). None of the things you do will be the most embarrassing things possible in your life, and you may find that the most limiting reaction is your own. We can control that by practicing going our own route. That route will lead to creativity.

Society often reinforces these personal limitations by convention, rules, and critical commentary. People question anything out of the ordinary, including efforts to be more creative. But creativity often needs to be a public act. Our creativity, in any form, needs to be shared with others. Think about new fashions, unique inventions, or other groundbreaking work that has defied convention and led to the future. For example, works by Miro were defaced and Stravinsky's *The Rite of Spring* was greeted with jeers and derision (Grout, 1973; Mink, 2000). Courage is often needed to be creative, particularly at first. We are often reticent about sharing our ideas and our work, but, in the end, that sharing allows our ideas to succeed and flourish.

Sometimes a creative act is one that others think is odd and raises questions. One method I've used in my classes is to instruct students in a magic phrase that puts most people at ease and lets students do something unusual or odd for their creativity exercises: "It's for class." Most people will step back and let you do what you're doing. They might ask about the class, and that's fine too, but this is one of the greatest excuses for acting unusual in public.

The Exercises

A lot of what happens in this book comes through a set of short exercises designed to encourage you to come up with different ideas. Just like the Alternative Uses Test in the previous chapter asked you to develop a number of different answers to a given "prompt" or starting point, these exercises will ask for many different responses to given words, images, or situations.

Doing the exercises repeatedly will help develop your ability to constantly come up with multiple, new ideas for any problem or situation. Usually we go through a set of ideas, and we edit and restrain our output. We hold back on ideas because they may seem silly, stupid, or weird. However, one rule for coming up with new ideas is to press forward with the sheer volume of ideas, regardless of how unusual they seem. At this point in solving a problem or answering a question, we're looking for as many ideas as possible. If you have difficulty having a lot of new ideas, just try to come up with bad ones. They're a lot more fun. Besides, this is a regular method for encouraging additional ideas.

In the creative fields, it's common to generate and develop multiple ideas for buildings, layouts, and solutions. Other cultures also support the idea of using multiple viewpoints as a matter of normal decision-making processes.

The other part, picking the best idea, is important as well. But, if you have a limited number of ideas from which to choose, the odds are that the final idea will be less creative and less productive.

Alternative Uses Test

We're going to do a brief exercise that is based on the Alternative Uses Test. We'll do these throughout the book, as they help develop the ability to generate a large number of answers in any situation. We'll be building the complexity of the prompt as we go along. Find something with which to write and something on which to write.

Most people are familiar with binder clips as a regular thing in many offices; you've probably used them in a number of different ways. Think of things that can be done with binder clips that are regular size, or large, or as big as a car. What could you do if you had a thousand binder clips delivered to your house? What would happen if they were different colors?

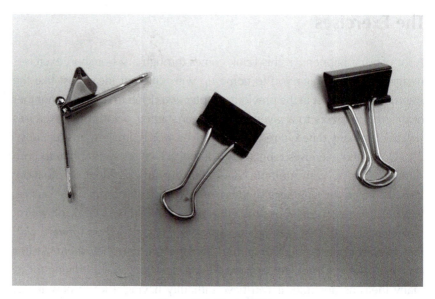

Figure 3.1 Binder Clips

You've got 90 seconds now to list everything you can do with binder clips like these, but of any size or description. Come up with as many ideas as you can. Remember, there are no wrong answers. Just try to come up with the largest number of different answers you can. If it helps, try to come up with those weird or unusual answers!

After you're done, count your answers. When this is done in my class, some people have a few answers, while others have many more. If you have only a few answers, have no fear, because we'll be practicing this exercise as we go through the book. And in doing so, you'll be able to increase the number of your responses. This is a measurement called fluency that refers to the ability to come up with a lot of answers.

I've seen responses that include chip-bag closers, really painful earrings, clothing adjustments, tie clips, a Barbie purse, a money clip, an exercise device for your fingers, and even a really large binder clip as a very large sculpture.

The Differents

Changing habits is a big change for anyone. And building a habit to consistently seek something different will require your thoughts and attention. You will need to consciously look at what you normally do, and then try to do something else. Like dieting, sticking to a budget, or quitting smoking, it's challenging to fight against our established pattern of behavior. That's why included in this book is a series of challenges to "Do Something Different." They're big, they're fun, and while they could be done quickly and easily, with more thought and invention, they can really change your outlook as well as your level of creativity.

The goal of this set of challenges is to get you to move past habits and self-imposed limitations and to develop the habit of trying new things, new adventures, and new ideas. Along with the smaller exercises in the book, these larger challenges will build your confidence, your creativity, and your courage.

When we were kids, we were less inhibited and, at the same time, less grown up. We were creative and sometimes did adventuresome things that our parents and others thought were inappropriate. We also developed biologically, and our brains became more conscious of what could go wrong and what we really should be doing. Unfortunately, this also cut down our capacity for creativity and innovation.

So we do need to consciously step past our set of boundaries. The Do Something Different exercises are ways to help us break past our self-imposed limits.

We probably don't learn to be creative in the privacy of our own bedroom, bathroom, or closet. For example, dancing around naked in your bathroom is not as challenging as dancing around fully clothed in a public space. It's not your dancing ability that is the challenge here, but rather the choice of a public venue that is most important, and possibly revealing.

First of all, each response to the assignment is to do something that is, for you, different. That means that if the challenge is to "wear something different," you won't be able to wear the same thing you did last Halloween on this Halloween. But you could wear it to work some otherwise normal day in February. And for the "eat something different," you can't eat the same old breakfast cereal in the same old way. But you could find some new and challenging way to eat it, like under water.

Your level of challenge has to be well understood because something that is easy for most people, such as eating Italian food or dressing up as a clown, might be extremely difficult for you. You have to make the challenge different from what you have done before, and your response should be at least a step beyond what is normal for you.

You should record your efforts and your process somewhere, like a journal. This written expression will help you think through your process and record your results. There is space in the book for recording this information, and you should include pictures to document your efforts. There are some general rules for each Do Something Different (DSD), as there are realistic limits to all of our challenges.

First, the DSD should not expose you to dangers that would result in serious and permanent harm. In other words, you can't jump off the biggest bridge in town because no one else has ever done it. There could be a strong chance of physical harm to yourself or others.

Second, you can't complete a DSD that would be harassing or demeaning to yourself or others.

And third, you cannot complete a DSD that would result in you being arrested and charged with an offense that carries with it penalties of 30 days in jail or more. Breaking the law is serious, and some crimes are much more serious than others. Jay-walking on a deserted street, for example, is probably less dangerous and less serious than a car theft, and it would not result in the same penalty. This will vary with locations.

You are responsible for your own actions in completing the Do Something Different assignments.

I hope you find these challenges worthwhile for your development as a more creative person and engaging as a learning experience.

Do Something Different: Eat

Now let's start the first of the larger challenges; these are called "Do Something Different" and should be done over the course of a week, from inspiration to completion, and done one at a time to focus your attention on the challenge at hand.

Your first challenge is to eat something different. Come up with a number of ideas and plan in advance what you're going to eat, and then carry out your plan. And then be open as your plan may change as you're doing it, recognizing that you might eat something *really* different. There are a couple of ways you can start to solve this challenge.

I'd suggest you first ask the question of what the term "eat" could mean. This is a great design-based model for generating a lot of ideas by looking at the problem and changing or redefining the challenge. So, first, try to figure out what the word "eat" means, or what it could be construed to mean. It could be used in the conventional sense, of accepting different forms of nourishment; or it could mean the process of eating rather than what you eat; or it could be a metaphor for other things, such as needing to "eat my hat" or "eat my words."

It could mean a lot of different things in a lot of different contexts, and that might give you a good idea as to how you could really eat something different.

You could also start by looking at food types or products that you've never eaten before, and understand that each possibility has within it some limitations. Your ethnic choices might include having Chinese food, but at the same time remember that it's not that unusual. We know that more than a billion people had Chinese food yesterday, so you should stretch that a little bit, or you can do something different when you get to a restaurant. There are also things you could eat that aren't regular food, such as paper or grass or things that are outside of your normal diet.

Secondly, you can eat in a way that's completely different from the ways you have before. We often sit down at a table in a restaurant or home in a well-lit room and use regular place settings, but that's not a permanent aspect of eating. You don't have to sit down at a table; you could stand up. You could eat in the dark, you could eat with only your fingers, or you could eat with your feet.

4 | Understanding Creativity

You can't use up creativity. The more you use, the more you have.

—Maya Angelou

I often get asked about what I teach. When I say I teach a class on creativity, there are three responses that generally happen in about the same order: First, people often say that creativity can't be defined; it's too unusual and ephemeral. Second, they say that since it can't be defined, it can't be evaluated. Finally, they say that creativity can't be taught. So while most people think positively about creativity as a skill, they often have difficulty defining it or seeing that it can be improved or evaluated.

While creativity is a complex phenomenon, there *is* a generally used definition of creativity. And in this chapter, we'll look more specifically at how creativity is defined and examine a couple of terms that are essential to better understanding creativity.

This will also give us a better understanding of how we can evaluate creativity and how it can be improved. In the previous chapters, we've started experiencing how creativity can be evaluated, through a series of challenges and quizzes, building on basic definitions of the term.

In later chapters, we'll see how we can build our own creativity as we increase knowledge and build our other skills. Most people recognize that with added schooling, intelligence can be increased; people learn to read and write, mathematics, chemistry, the scientific method, or the realm of the law. Research has also shown that through sustained effort, we can learn and we can become more creative. Character strengths or skills such as creativity develop over time and can be increased through practice, through the introduction of skills, by changing our habits, and this effort is enabled by a belief in one's ability to change and improve (Petersen & Seligman, 2004). We must recognize that everyone has the capacity to be creative, and that capacity can be improved, just as knowledge can be improved through education. That is the goal of this book.

One way to begin understand creativity is to look at the historical aspects of creativity, examining those famous people who were considered to be creative, often focusing our attention on the arts or on scientists/inventors.

Historic v. Psychological, Individual v. Societal

What people do you know of in your community that *are* creative? Maybe they're not famous, but they may be inventive or creative in their own way.

When people talk about creativity, they often mention very creative and famous people such as Einstein, Picasso, or Beethoven. This way of describing creativity is called "big C" creativity. The premise of "big C" creativity is that we can learn about creativity by examining those who have demonstrated their skill in new ways, with notoriety in their field being an indicator of creative talent. This narrows our understanding of creativity to mastery of specific fields or domains, and is one that is strongly tied to intelligence.

We can also examine creativity in other ways. We can examine how the individual is creative in everyday life. This is called "little c" creativity. It includes those who are creative without being famous—people whose work requires creative ideas and development, but who have not changed their field or domain. Not everyone will be famous and recognized for "big C" status, but having more "little c" creative talents in society will lead to more and more "big C" creatives. How many potentially creative people are there? At least seven billion.

Here we're focusing on our own creativity: the development of creativity for application in everyday life, and across our many endeavors. Everyone can be more creative, building on his or her innate human talent and skill. It is creativity for the rest of us. Creativity for all. Quotidian creativity. This is often referred to as "little c" creativity for everyday life, where creativity can be employed in any field or domain.

Developing the creativity of individuals will have a long-lasting effect on the health of society at large, benefits that are in addition to improving the well-being of each individual. And that, too, is the focus of this book.

Defining Creativity

When asked how he got good creative ideas, two-time Nobel Prize winner Linus Pauling said: "The best way to have a good idea is to have a lot of ideas and then to throw the bad ones away."

That simple observation can help us understand, as well as develop, our own creativity. And it is close, in essence, to the broadly held definition of creativity that is used by researchers and educators (Runco & Jaeger, 2012).

Creativity is the ability to generate and express ideas that are *new and useful* or, in other words, *novel and applicable.* It could also be described as the production of something *original and worthwhile.* While this basic and common definition isn't highly technical and researchers have diverged dramatically in examining the nuances of creativity, this common understanding remains generally held, and it is widely used by research organizations such as the National Science Foundation.

Many people often confuse "creativity" and "innovation." The two terms are often interchanged; in reality, they are different concepts. Creativity is the development of new and useful ideas; innovation is the *application,* or use, of a new idea. This could include the acceptance of a new product by the general public, or the adoption of new neighborhood habits for the prevention of crime. It is "the successful adoption of new ideas" (Cox, 2005). Most of what is dealt with in this book does not address innovation, for creativity precedes innovation.

Creative ideas are ideas that are (either in whole or in a specific context) new, and they can be applied to a challenge at hand, appropriate to the specific context.

What's the difference between applicable and appropriate? Both provide a means to evaluate all the novel and divergent ideas that are possible, but there may be subtle differences. "Applicable" seems to be targeted at something that can be put to use directly, whereas "appropriate" appears to be something that is acceptable by society. We can use both in our pursuit of becoming more creative.

This basic definition is one that is broad ranging and useful in all fields. While simple, it leads to how we can understand and improve our own creativity.

Let's first look at the aspect of being useful and applicable and see how these terms can inform our becoming more creative.

Applicable

The term "applicable" is most focused on finding an answer or something that can be put to use. The evaluation of useful, applicable, or appropriate often relies on knowledge or expertise in a discipline. One needs to know about the discipline to select and improve a given idea. Skilled architects or fashion designers bring their understanding of aesthetics, function, and materials to their work; similarly, biologists and businesspeople also use their research and understanding to select ideas for development. Each field of study and each area of expertise has its own base of knowledge and judgment. It is the essential aspect of the second part of Pauling's comment: "you throw the bad ones away." So a question would be: How do you know what the bad ones are? Through your own experience and learned expertise, and this is our evaluation of ideas for their quality.

Creativity in disciplines or areas of study often needs to fit in an existing structure based on the knowledge and understanding of the field. Of course, that structure also often encourages the status quo and supports current ideas and theories. Inherently, this aspect of the process is more conservative than generative. This type of thinking, called *convergent thinking*, is meant to select the best answer and to improve that single idea.

There is a balance that is necessary for creativity, particularly in terms of convergent thinking. Knowledge of the field or context is needed, and yet it could also be limiting to creative efforts. To play jazz or to perform improv, one needs to know how to use the structure, and not to memorize the components.

Assumptions and Constraints

Out of the box

One of the most clichéd descriptions of creativity is the term "thinking outside the box." Using the same term to describe the process of coming up with different ideas and ways of looking at things is ironic. It does have a basis in creativity and assumptions. The term is based on a drawing problem of connecting nine dots with straight lines; it cannot be completed if the assumption is to remain within the box of nine dots (see Exercise 4.1).

In most cases in our own lives, we're very good at doing something that is useful or applicable—whether it's our job or picking something for dinner. We need only to do the same old thing. We find one answer that can work, remember the way we did it before, and follow the same process. Improvement is minimal at best, but we don't have to think about what we're doing or to make difficult choices, because we're doing things that are the *same*. We have a modest degree of variety, with little cognitive effort.

Something that is not the same could be described as unusual, or, if it's new, it could also be considered original. That's our goal with creativity, to move past the ordinary and to something that's original and, if need be, unusual. It requires additional mental effort to go beyond our regular habits.

We all self-edit and limit our possible answers to any question. We've matured and often recognize the limits of our own actions. However, many people are limited by social pressure and habit. We also seek to find the single correct answer. Unfortunately, in most cases, there are a number of possible answers that are never considered. We make assumptions, limiting ourselves as to what could and couldn't be a solution.

Exercise 4.1: The Nine-Dot Problem

Connect the nine dots with four connected straight lines without lifting your pencil from the paper.

Outside of our personal lives, we are often also constrained by our society, our jobs, or our schools. Many organizations have structures that

Figure 4.1 The Nine-Dot Problem

control possible outcomes and that might limit creativity. People can be creative in almost any situation, but the outcome and scale of that creativity will vary. Being in an open and engaging culture is obviously the most supportive place for creativity, but one's context may be restrictive or conservative. Working within a limiting context is a challenge for each individual.

Similarly, often our own assumptions constrain our ideas. We make assumptions about what can and can't be done or what is possible and what the challenges really are. An important easy lesson about being creative is to examine the initial problem to be solved and to redefine that problem and the limits that we ourselves put on any problem.

Imagine, for example, a scenario and anticipate what you can and can't do. What are your self-imposed limits as to what you can eat, who you can talk to, or what you can wear?

Novel and Original

Children are generally viewed as more creative and less inhibited in coming up with new ideas. We eventually learned to play by the rules, fit in our social setting, got used to school, and became more mature. We have learned to look for the one correct answer and be satisfied when we found it. We became more efficient, but at a loss in creativity. In creativity research and in terms of divergent thinking, this is often called the "fourth grade slump." (Torrance, 1968)

Our ideas and our answers are often correct but not new, because when we search for an answer and find an answer that is workable, we stop. Simon (1978) called this "satisficing"—i.e., getting something that is good enough.

In terms of creativity, however, the only *wrong* answer is *one* answer. Because that's where we often stop seeking answers, and it's often the answer from before.

How, then, do you come up with more "new" or "original" ideas? The most obvious way is to develop a large number of ideas. As we know through research, having more ideas will lead us to more "original" ideas (Osborn, 1963; Goldschmidt & Tatsa, 2005; Kudrowitz & Wallace, 2013). That aspect of creativity, called divergent thinking, can be developed through training—that is, practice in coming up with a wide range of answers.

This, of course, connects directly with the first half of that Linus Pauling quote: "have a lot of ideas." Having a lot of ideas leads you to having ideas that are original and unusual, often after the normal ideas have already been presented. To have a lot of ideas, we need to get past immediately evaluating ideas for quality and need to seek a large number of possible choices. This leads us to practice generating new and novel ideas.

Toothbrushing Exercise

One way to build your creative capacity is to exercise your creativity on a regular basis. A good way to do this is to piggy-back on other patterns or habits and make creative skills stronger. A positive habit most people have is to brush their teeth on a regular basis. We do this a number of times a day: when we get up, when we we're getting ready for bed, and sometimes after we've eaten something spicy and we're going to be close to other people.

Dentists often say that we should brush longer, and they suggest singing a tune while brushing. There are children's toothbrushes that play a tune to keep kids brushing. So, as a new habit, let's try practicing our divergent thinking. The next time you're brushing your teeth, spot something in the bathroom and think of ten different things you could do with that object, and keep brushing until you come up with ten new uses. The thing you work with could be a towel, a drinking glass, or someone else's toothbrush. The object you're thinking about doesn't matter; it's just a starting point. For example, you could use the toothbrush to clean up the faucet, or you could use the towel as a cape. Now think of ten things that are different from its original intended use.

You'll brush longer at the beginning as you develop your thinking skills. Over time, you'll get better at coming up with unusual uses while cleaning your teeth. As you generate ideas, your teeth will be cleaner as well. You'll also practice your ability to develop a large number of different and interesting ideas, which will help you even when you're not brushing your teeth.

Alternative Uses

We'll again do a brief exercise that is based on the Alternative Uses Test. This is a simple exercise that, when repeated, will help us build our skills in developing divergent ideas.

Most people use pencils and have used them in a number of different ways. Think of things that can be done with pencils that are regular size or as big as a tree. What could you do if you had a thousand pencils delivered to your house? Or if you got one really large pencil in the mail?

Exercise 4.2: Alternative Uses Exercise

Use 90 seconds now to list everything you can do with pencils. Come up with as many ideas as you can, and, of course, there are no wrong answers. Come up with the largest number of different answers you can.

And after you're done, count your answers. This measures your ability to produce new or novel ideas.

1. _____

2. _____

3. _____

4. _____

5. _____

6. _____

7. _____

8. _____

9. _____

10. _____

11. _____

12. _____

13. _____

14. _____

15. _____

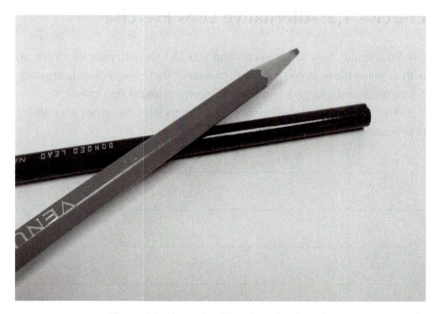

Figure 4.2 Alternative Uses Exercise: Pencils

Of particular interest are the answers beyond the first one, because these hold the best chance for being divergent or different. To get a creative answer, we'd just need to be lucky with the first answer we develop. The problem is that they don't arrive in random order; the most mentally privileged, regular answers come first, and the new, original, and unusual answers come later, but because the current, well-used answers are easily accepted, they often aren't even developed.

Research shows that the initial answers that are given for any question are those that are most common and expected (see, for example, Diehl & Stroebe, 1987; Kudrowitz & Wallace, 2013). Later answers are more original or novel. If ideas came randomly, there would be no need to generate a lot of answers in finding a good new idea; we often make assumptions about challenges or problems we face, or about choices we make, without attempting alternatives. We work within a given problem space, accept one of a few possible answers, and do not reach out for better alternatives.

Of course, new ideas aren't *necessarily* useful; they are ideas that could be strange, different, off-beat, outlandish, weird, or just slightly new but not useful. However, as part of the creative process, they need to be accepted as *possible* by those generating the ideas and considered for potential application. Application and acceptance by experts or society at large will evaluate the ideas for their value and relative merit, but, initially, new ideas must be first *considered* as having potential merit. To be creative is to delay judgment and to accept that unusual, untried, or controversial ideas can have value. We must not limit our ideas by our assumptions as to what could work.

We all make assumptions about what we can do and what we can't do, about our own abilities and capability. And if we decide ahead of time that we aren't creative, we will be less creative. Choosing to seek to be creative will involve trying new things and generating more ideas and will eventually lead to recognition of our creativity. Many times the constraints we put on our creativity are placed there by ourselves, and we fail to contest or ignore external constraints as well.

A Small Part of Cognitive Science

A lot of our understanding of creativity in general, and specifically our own personal creativity, is shaped by a number of assumptions most people hold. People have an opinion about how creative they are, based on life experience. They often claim that they aren't artists or aren't involved in a creative job and that, therefore, they are not creative. Or they have been told they are not creative. Most adults often believe their creative skill is fixed and low or non-existent, that they are constrained and limited to a given level. Research, however, shows that creativity can be improved and is not fixed.

Where do new ideas come from? They are caused by connections and combinations inside the brain that are often influenced by a lot of things from the outside. We start in solving problems by reviewing and remembering our past experiences, whether novel or common, and begin solutions based on what we've done or seen. Many times we use well-worn paths to solve problems, routes that require less mental effort and that end in the same results.

We search our memory for different answers and develop ideas from that set of resources. Our memory resources have been filled by our diverse experiences and learning, and how they interact can give us directions for our creativity.

We may be spurred to develop new ideas by different forms of problems, by inspiration from external influences, or by conscious effort (Epstein, 1996). There are the resources we have in our own mind—our experience and knowledge—but we often need a little nudge to make the connections. A lot of times, new ideas or concepts are formed by putting different ideas, "schemas," together.

What we know and remember can be combined in different ways; ordinarily, our mind maintains things in order, but when "disassociated" we can make more unusual connections. If we're consciously reminded to seek more original answers, either by dictate or by training, we may apply methods to encourage the development of different ideas.

Creativity research by Martindale (1999) studied the development of ideas and found three general parts: letting loose or becoming "disassociated," having sufficient raw mental material to combine into new ideas, and developing a large number of possible combinations. A three-step model in improving creativity could include becoming more open to divergent or ambiguous answers, having a wide range of mental options for possible use, and having a practice of generating a lot of idea combinations.

That first aspect, becoming more accepting to divergent ideas, is a soft skill that runs contrary to our development and maturation. As mature adults, our frontal lobes organize brain activity, limiting or allowing the exploration of divergent ideas, ideas that "take a different direction from the prevailing modes of thought or expression" (Heilman et al., 2003). Generally, creatives need the ability to accept divergent views or to make unusual connections between different mental systems.

Younger children haven't developed this maturity yet, as part of the maturation of children affects the control centers of the brain. This can limit, along with social pressure, their ability to be more creative.

In general, scientists also believe that creative ideas are sparked when different parts of the brain interact, generating a new "idea." Idea generation often occurs across different parts of the brain via connecting neural pathways (Gabora, 2002). As we focus on workable ideas, we narrow our mental search (Kudrowitz & Wallace, 2013). By remaining open to new ideas, we can develop new and alternative pathways by practice.

Much of this book focuses on the skill to develop a lot of ideas; multiple ideas will provide us with more choices and, in the end, better ideas. The other components of becoming more creative are also important, and what we can also start with is continuing a practice of developing new experiences and in moving past our personal boundaries, assumptions, and limits. We'll do this with our next Do Something Different.

Do Something Different

One research- and personally-based observation of creativity is that children are often more spontaneous and creative before they are socialized by the educational process (see, for example, Torrance, 1968; or Land & Jarman, 1993). In other words, you *played* as a kid but do not as much now as an adult. You've experienced the "fourth grade slump" in your own creativity.

Think back to some of your own childhood experiences, and, for this DSD, do something you used to do as a child that you don't do now. You can be creative based on your choice, your reasoning, and your reflections of change between then and now. Again, record your activity with photos and writing.

5 | Modes of Thinking

Creativity is allowing yourself to make mistakes. Art is knowing which ones to keep.

—Scott Adams

In the field of creativity, we often speak about two different types of thinking: *convergent* and *divergent*. Both are needed in problem solving and derive from our initial definition of creativity. The two components are the generation of new ideas (via divergent thinking) and evaluation of these ideas (via convergent thinking).

Diverse thinking can be described as a thought process or method that is used to generate creative ideas by exploring many possible solutions. Diverging from the single initial idea is the most important aspect; the key here is in generating multiple ideas and in the development of novelty.

Convergent thinking, in contrast, is the process of developing one solution, often through a logical process. It does focus on a single answer, and it makes that answer better through critique, additional creative ideas, or hard work. In the area of convergent thinking, knowledge is of particular importance: It is a source of ideas, suggests pathways to implementation, and provides criteria of effectiveness and novelty (what works and what is original).

One of the most obvious differences between intelligence and creativity is that intelligence requires convergent thinking, coming up with the single right answer, while creativity requires divergent thinking, coming up with many potential answers.

(Sawyer, 2011, p. 46)

Remembering which type of thinking can be derived from the regular use of the words "divergent" and "convergent." If you are following a path, and the path splits into three dimensions, it is said to diverge. If you come to a meeting place, where all the paths come together, they are said to converge. If you follow the same path, you will get to the same location. Taking a different path in the woods or life will lead to different and creative results.

A real-life example can be used to illustrate the different modes of creative thinking. As they are growing up, many people date many different people. This is like having a lot of different ideas to solve any problem, and it is like divergent thinking. Many times a person finds someone special and builds a long-term relationship with him or her. This can be comparable to selecting one idea and improving that idea. To carry the metaphor further, like real life, sometimes we make a wrong choice and need to start over . . . or we have difficulty in making an initial choice. To build you creativity, you need to "date" a number of different ideas before you settle down with just one.

Divergent Thinking

While a balance is needed between convergent and divergent thinking, this book focuses on divergent thinking, or the ability to generate a variety of ideas. This is for a number of reasons: First, if you learn to generate a lot of new ideas, you'll have faster results and have an earlier impact than if you focused on painstakingly improving the same old idea. Second, our current educational system focuses on convergent thinking that is seeking a single correct answer while discouraging divergent thinking. "Teachers tend to discriminate against highly creative students, labeling them as troublemakers. In response, many children quickly learn to get with the program, keeping their original ideas to themselves" (Grant, 2016, p. 10). Third, as convergent thinking is more discipline specific, development in divergent thinking can be applied to a broader range of fields. Finally, the skills of divergent thinking are integrated into the logical processes of convergent thinking, including such aspects as redefining or finding problems, courage, a sense of experimentation, and multiple answers or paths.

The exercises in this book focus on divergent thinking and on developing the variability of answers. As most education today focuses on using a logical, linear work process and convergent methods to find a single solution, divergent thinking is, by contrast, where transformative ideas and change can develop. And while much of convergent thinking is linear and doctrinaire, it still relies on a continuous flow of alternatives and experimentation.

There are two guiding ideas behind this exercise focus. First, through practice, we'll become more rapid in our thinking and build the ability to create multiple ideas. And, second, we will develop our ability to suspend judgment and examine a wider range of ideas.

This aspect of creativity is divergent thinking. Its central tenet is that you shouldn't stop at the very first idea you come up with for any given problem. Divergent thinking is how to see lots of possible answers to a question, how to interpret a question in many ways, how to think non-linearly, and how to find more original answers (Robinson, 2010).

Divergent thinking involves producing multiple or alternative answers from available information. It requires making unexpected combinations, recognizing links among remote associates, transforming information into unexpected forms, and the like (Cropley, 2006, p. 391).

Divergent thinking is thinking that seeks multiple and unusual answers and ideas for any given problem. If you generate more ideas, you might discover ideas that are interesting, amusing, or even earth-shattering. For many artists and composers, having a lot of ideas corresponds to producing more work that is important in their field. Beethoven, Bach, Shakespeare, and Prince all were prolific and generated substantial amounts of work, which correlates with the extreme level of their most significant creative works. Similar creative development occurs in the sciences, with highly generative authors producing the most breakthrough articles (Simonton, 1997). As Pauling said, "The best way to have a good idea is to have a lot of ideas and then to throw the bad ones away."

One of the main goals of this book is to develop your skill in generating multiple ideas and to instill in you the idea that the only wrong answer is one answer. We all need to be able to come up with more than one answer, and preferably many answers, to any given problem, and that's the main lead as to why we focus on divergent thinking.

One of the main constraints in developing a lot of ideas is our own brain, and our maturity. We know what other people expect, what society often wants, and the fact that there are wrong answers. In the generation of new ideas, the categories of expected, wanted, and wrong don't matter. We need to go past our own limiting thoughts and controlling judgments and find ideas that are unusual and that might be considered weird or absurd.

Convergent Thinking

The second aspect of our initial quote from Linus Pauling, keeping and improving the good ideas, is called convergent thinking.

Convergent thinking is oriented toward deriving the single best (or correct) answer to a clearly defined question. It emphasizes speed, accuracy, and logic; it focuses on recognizing the familiar, reapplying set techniques, and accumulating information. Therefore, it is most effective in situations where a readymade answer exists and needs simply to be recalled from stored information or worked out from what is already known by applying conventional and logical search, recognition, and decision-making strategies. One of the most important aspects of convergent thinking is that it leads to a single best answer and, thus, leaves no room for ambiguity: Answers are either right or wrong. Convergent thinking is also intimately linked to knowledge: On the one hand, it involves manipulation of existing knowledge by means of standard procedures, and, on the other hand, its main result is production of increased knowledge.

Most of the experience we have in education can be seen as being focused on what is called convergent thinking. It seeks the single best answer for a challenge and to utilize established methods and information to reach solutions. While convergent thinking is not focused on the development of different and unusual ideas, it seeks to improve existing ideas and to select among various ideas the best possible solution. It's strongly based on a knowledge of the area, and it uses that knowledge to make informed judgments. "Convergent thinking usually generates orthodoxy, whereas divergent thinking always generates variability" (Cropley, 2006, p. 392).

How does one select and improve the one idea from many? By applying existing knowledge and judgments about the situation. Within any given field of study, there is knowledge regarding information, procedures, and skills. As it's difficult to include all areas of study in a single book, here we are using our own lives, lived experience as the domain for creativity. Being creative in real life can lead to creativity in our field of student or professional practice.

Being creative in any field will require using the elements of the field, both the explicit and the implicit ones, to advance a new and useful idea. For example, when learning tango, many students rigidly learn a set of steps or figures. They repeat these figures when social dancing and are recognized to have only one aspect of the full knowledge of the dance. The skills of movement and musicality add much to the dance experience and come from extensive work in the field. But they don't come from knowing the steps. Creativity within tango can come from unusual moves or figures or from the personal choreography of combining steps and sequences.

An important part of convergent thinking is the evaluation and improvement of an existing idea.

Using Both Modes of Thinking

To some extent, all the end responses from the DSDs result from both divergent and convergent thinking, often moving back and forth between the two. One can imagine a mental conversation between divergent thinking and convergent thinking when it comes to completing one of the Do Something Differents:

> Divergent Thinking: Here are eight ideas for the project. [Multiple ideas are generated.]
>
> Convergent Thinking: Number 7 has nothing to do with the project. [It's not applicable; it doesn't work.]
>
> CT: I've done 1, 2, and 4, so the others are new for me. [Ideas are evaluated by whether they are "different" or not.]
>
> CT: Number 5 seems to take the least effort, but it's dull; number 6 looks interesting, but it could be embarrassing for me. Number 6 works best for my goal of "learn something," but I need to make it less embarrassing.
>
> DT: Here are a couple of ways to do that. [The initial idea is improved—elaboration.]

The Last Place You Look

There is one rhetorical question that is often asked when searching for something you have misplaced: "Why is it always in the last place you look?" Logically, of course, it is because most people have a very simple goal in mind when searching—i.e., to find the single lost object. When that goal is reached, we've completed the task, and we stop. We generally aren't trying to accomplish anything further. It is an objective judgment; either it's found or it's not. However, if it's a subjective question that must be evaluated through judgment and experience, we do need to do more.

If we have other goals for the searching, seeking more than a simple object, the search will continue beyond finding the first result. And, metaphorically, as we're searching for ideas, we need to search past one answer to get better results.

If we can't find a specific object, we also logically look where it should be, and then where we saw it last.

For example, if we need a shirt to wear and almost any will do, then the first shirt will be acceptable. In an emergency, any shirt works. However, if our goal is to find a clean shirt, or a blue shirt, it becomes more complex, but it is still a directly solvable problem. If we're searching for the *best* shirt to complete our outfit, it requires evaluation of a range of different criteria, and finding the "right" result could include finding many different shirts and trying many options. So when we're seeking a creative solution, the first idea to complete the simplest task is not enough. We need to go beyond and explore different types of ideas.

So, to develop your creative skills, the next time you search for something, try looking in more places where it could be, even though it's already been found. Why wasn't it in the later places? What else did you find there instead? Importantly, where are you looking?

Solution Space

Problems and their solutions are sometimes thought of in terms of space and location. They are described as being part of a "problem space." The possible answers or solutions can be within a "solution space." Both can be graphic representations of the limits for possible answers to a given problem.

Of the two terms, "solution space" seems to be a more appropriate concept as something that covers all possible solutions that the problem solver might consider. Boundaries of a solution are set by constraints due to limited experience, knowledge, or perceptions of the problem solver.

People tend to select uncreative ideas early in problem-solving processes, based on their own habits and preferences, and they won't seek further or divergent possibilities.

Usually, people select the first answer they come up with and many times they use the default answer, the answer that's been given to them. It's moving the shortest distance to make a choice. This can be seen in our naïve acceptance of privacy defaults for Facebook and new software, and in our setting retirement contributions the same as everyone else at work places. The first answer we find seems to work reasonably well, and, in reality, we usually stick with that initial choice. It's merely selecting a relatively satisfactory answer, which is called "satisficing."

In Diagram 5.1, we see the one choice: We are trying to get from the problem or prompt (in our case, "eat something") to actually eating something. We often pick the first answer at hand. We don't try to find others, unless the first one doesn't work out. Here we can see some of the alternatives.

In reality, there are many possible solutions to most complex problems, and they can be described as being part of a "solution space," where ideas that could work are included. Within the solution space, there are a number of possible ideas for solving the problem or challenge—where ideas are feasible, possible, attainable, workable.

Most times we simply go for the first idea, the first solution, but, once we see there are a number of possible or feasible choices, we can choose others.

Some ideas are more challenging than others; they are less easy to implement, because of our own choices or because of cultural or physical limitations. Some may approach the boundary of what is "feasible," or the

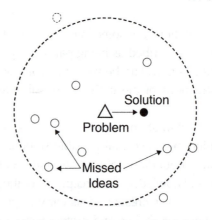

Diagram 5.1 Initial Solution Space, Expanded Solution Space, and Experimental Solution Space

limits of the solution space. And some ideas *are* easier, less challenging, or less difficult. They are represented by being closer to the initial challenge. If we look at the distance from the problem to the idea, this can also represent ideas that are more or less difficult to implement. It gives a graphic representation of an idea that is "far out."

Seeking more creative and divergent solutions necessitates looking closer to the edge of what is commonly accepted.

At the same time, we need to recognize that the limits of the solution space are generated by our understanding of the problem (see Diagram 5.2). The limits of solutions are perceived, not real. Others may have different limits on what they can do, and we can consciously change the limits ourselves. This is a "perceived" solution space, one that our functional and personal limits form, and there is an "actual" solution space, with possible answers. The actual solution space may be much larger than what we assume or perceive. There are some things that are outside of *our* perceived solution space by our choice but that are realistic solutions, such as eating mayonnaise (for me) or eating completely naked (which is difficult in public) or eating your hat (as it's difficult to admit you are wrong at any time).

Greater knowledge of any problem helps us expand our solution space, and convergent thinking helps us to select better and possible answers. We can understand what things are possible and which ideas are better by developing knowledge of the context.

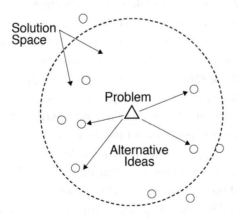

Diagram 5.2 Developing Multiple Ideas within a Solution Space

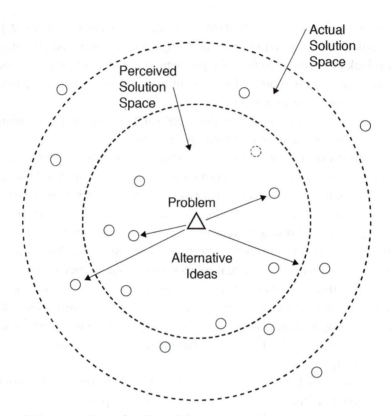

Diagram 5.3 Expanding the Solution Space to Develop More Answers

Creativity often comes from stretching the possible solution space or redefining or changing the problem. If we change the definition of the problem (as we could), we will also change the solution space.

There is a range of expected answers to any given problem or question, a solution space that is understood; some answers are better than others, while, at the same time, those solutions that are just outside the solution space often get ignored or rejected automatically. Just like the old phrase "pushing the envelope," but in a more conceptual realm, we all need to go past the expected boundaries. And, importantly, we need to expand our solution space. This also means there is a realm of ideas that could be considered "experimental" that are beyond what would normally be acceptable. These are ideas beyond our own solution space. Similarly, we can represent different categories or concepts of solutions as segments of the solution space. See Diagram 5.4.

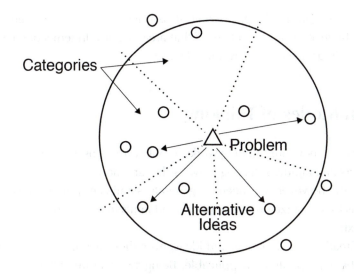

Diagram 5.4 Finding Alternative Solutions in Different Solution Space Categories

The solution space of a design problem involved knowledge from a variety of domains. The body of knowledge and its interrelations present in and directly accessible to the designer, e.g., retrieved from long-term memory while studying the design brief can be described as the initial solutions space. However, the complexity of most design problems requires gathering additional information, either from domains closely related to the problem at hand or even from domains that have never been related to this particular problem before. Thus, the final solution space expands from the initial solution space and includes information extent and memory and knowledge learned from new information. Productive thinking, i.e. restructuring the information in the final solution space can lead to creative solutions to the novel design problem.

(Shackleton & Sugiyama, 1998, p. 168)

In this book, we have learned to be creative by doing things that will help you try out divergent ideas at the cost of being a little different and possibly embarrassed. We often put limits on ourselves as to what we can try or what we propose as a new idea. The major impact is on divergent thinking, holding back on the instant choices of convergent thinking and the drive to get things done.

Convergent thinking, in contrast, is driven by the knowledge of the field, the theories and practices of that area of study. In terms of creativity, you don't just need *done. You need more.*

Both Modes of Thinking

We can see how our thinking works in both directions, searching for more answers and rapidly selecting answers that are more workable. To develop creativity, however, we need to generate significantly more answers as well as to recognize our assumptions and limits imposed artificially by our context.

Creativity is a balance, and ideas, even those that are highly original, must be appropriate and applicable. Being aware of the different kinds of thinking, and understanding both types of creative thinking, will help in our efforts to be more creative.

Do Something Different

Plan beforehand, and implement something completely different that your roommate or significant other (spouse, lover, etc.) always does that you don't (ever). Record your experience (why it is completely different, what you planned, and the results). Note also that you may need to do this for a significant period of time, as it needs to be appropriate for the activity. Write it down, and add photos to record your effort. The goal is to get pictures that capture the essence of differentness; describe why this is different from what you usually do and why this is the same as what the other person does.

6 | **Evaluating Creativity**

> Creativity comes from looking for the unexpected and stepping outside your own experience.
>
> —Masaru Ibuka

Introduction

In this book you've been asked to try some timed tasks that help you understand, in one way, how creative you are. Though not perfect, tests like these are widely used in creativity research and can provide some idea of how creative you are. There are other ways to evaluate your creativity based on what you have done and what you usually do. However, the goal of this book is to use the simpler, more pragmatic methods of evaluating general creativity and originality to help better understand creativity.

In the beginning of the book, you took a brief test of your abilities to generate ideas and concepts. Scoring of the test gave you a couple of different numbers: the first being the total number of answers you had to the given prompts or triggers, and the second counting the times you came up with unexpected answers.

As we've seen earlier, the ability to develop of a lot of different responses to a question is called *fluency*. It's the most basic measurement of creativity and is the simplest to score. You count all the answers that deal with the challenge, whether it's things you can do with a brick or the advantages of having your car stolen.

Time is a limiting factor in testing fluency, as the rapidity of response is part of the essence of creativity. If you had unlimited time, it wouldn't matter when you came up with a good answer, be it five minutes or five years from now. But most tests (and real life) have time limits. In testing and evaluation, this sets a reasonable upper level on the number of answers received. In our case, the average number of answers that people develop over three minutes is about nine.

Originality

Research has shown, however, that when people develop more than ten answers, their later answers are more original and unusual. This is the second basic measurement in creativity: *originality*. This may be the most important aspect of creativity, going past raw numbers of ideas to discover their uniqueness. Ideas that are the same as those that are currently used may be effective, but we are trying to find answers that are different and original.

This is kind of a reverse test and unlike most other tests you take. The goal is not to get the single right answer; it's to get many of the *other* answers that are possible, those that could happen, and those that are original. Original answers are those that are either very rare (say, being less than 5% of the responses possible from society at large) or unique (that is, answers that were not given by anyone else). Logically, these are more unusual than the commonly given answers, but then, if we wanted the same answers, we wouldn't need to be creative. In order for an answer to be original, and therefore creative, it needs first to be different; *the same* can be considered the opposite of *creative*.

These divergent answers may also be the answers that are the most valuable, those that no one else has pursued or expressed (Sternberg & Lubart, 1999). It's important to remember that original quote from Linus Pauling about having many ideas. Research also shows that those recognized as great artists or composers or inventors generate a greater number of ideas, and, while they have masterpieces, they also have produced significantly more works in their lifetimes (Simonton, 1997). For example, Einstein wrote over 200 published papers in his life, but three of the early papers are viewed as changing modern physics. Edison held over 1,000 patents for inventions, but only a handful were world-changing, or even profitable. Mozart wrote over 600 compositions, but only five are considered essential to the canon. The Rolling Stones as composers also have a large musical library; some songs are famous, while some songs are seldom performed. Their strength in creativity comes through their extensive generation of new work.

So that's why we start with "different" in an effort to be more creative. "Different" is the easiest defining characteristic of any effort seeking to be creative. In order to improve an answer or process, something must change, and, if we are seeking transformative results, our changes must be more substantial: "Original thinkers will come up with many ideas that are strange mutations, dead ends, and utter failures. The cost is worthwhile because they generate a larger pool of ideas—especially novel ideas" (Sutton, 2002, p. 36).

This leads back to the concept of "the only wrong answer is one" because usually that one answer is exclusive, eliminating all other answers. That one answer is conclusive, stopping the development of all other possible alternatives. It eliminates the possibility of choice and varied opinion. The subjective judging of which idea is most "original" is turned to an objective decision as to whether or not the single answer or not will work. If not, then another idea is sought; no qualitative evaluation is undertaken, and, similarly, ideas are not judged as to their novelty. The need to be creative implies the need for different answers, different problems, and different approaches to solve problems.

Flexibility

One other aspect of creativity that can be tested using a similar method is called *flexibility*. This is seen to seek answers that go beyond slight differences and to generate new answers that are categorically different from those previously given. For example, when asked what they could eat, sometimes people mentioned "pizza." There are all different types of pizza: cheese, sausage, pepperoni, veggie, etc. All of these answers would be considered responses that count toward a fluency evaluation. But all are of the same type of food and so would be in the same category, variations of the same food type, so the originality would be low.

Different types of answers—or categories—can open you to different directions for answers, and this helps encourage even more original ideas. To develop our flexibility, we need to consciously diversify the kinds of answers we propose, the different categories of answers for any challenge.

One way to develop different types of answers or practice generating a wide range of ideas is to respond to a category or concept; for example, "things one could find in the trunk of a car" could include a spare tire, a tire iron, gloves, battery cables, a snow shovel, a suitcase, groceries from the store, or tacos that were long forgotten. As with the Alternative Uses Test, our list of what we find in the trunk often begins with those things that are most likely, and it proceeds to more unusual and creative items. If we generate a lot of possible answers, we will have more divergent responses.

Categories

These answers can be ranked as being important or not. Consider "things you take with you if your house is on fire" or "what to bring for a trip to the beach." In both cases, you'd have a good idea of things that would be critical to bring with you and things that would be good but not that valuable. For example, you'd probably grab the irreplaceable family photos when you leave the burning house, but not a beach blanket. And few people would think to bring the beach umbrella when fleeing a fire. This is a demonstration of convergent thinking. We make our choices based on our experience, knowledge, and the situation. You are choosing based on logical decisions. You've generated ideas, with probably the most common ideas at the beginning of your list. Those that are less frequently thought of only come later. Reviewing the list and moving items up or down by importance is an example of convergent thinking. You are making judgments as to the relative value of each item.

If we examine unusual categories, we'll be pushed to more thoughtful and divergent answers, and this will work as a good exercise for developing our own creativity. Here are some additional categories that could be used:

- things you pack when you go on a quick vacation to Cleveland
- things that are usually forgotten in the back of a taxi
- objects that cost less than $10 at a flea market.

Let's explore one category and see the range of answers we can develop, and let's also begin to work on our convergent thinking by ranking the answers.

Exercise 6.1: Categories

Things you should *not* bring with you when you go camping:

1. _____

2. _____

3. _____

4. _____

5. _____

6. _____

7. _____

8. _____

9. _____

10. _____

11. _____

12. _____

13. _____

14. _____

15. _____

After you've completed the list, rank your ideas, with the most important item listed as number 1.

Which is the most unusual item on the list? Is it one of the final items? That may indicate how much more divergent you need to be to complete such a large list.

Elaboration

We also need to edit and improve our answers, adding diverse details and building our understanding of each new idea. It is an aspect of creativity.

Another common way to evaluative creativity is to examine how details have been added to an initial idea. This might be in terms of how the idea is applied or implemented, of what materials might be used, or of what problems might exist with the idea—or, for that matter, how the idea is made more interesting or aesthetically pleasing. To move any idea forward will require a number of details to be explained, and the more details, the more thought-out the idea, and the more creative idea generation has occurred.

The Consequences Test in Chapter 2 is built on this idea of developing details beyond the original idea. There, for a fast evaluation, we counted the details added to each different idea.

These simple methods can help us understand our current capability for creativity. The tasks were created to isolate certain characteristics and to be individually completed. The Do Something Different exercises can also be evaluated by the number of ideas considered (fluency), the details of the ideas and implementation (elaboration), and the uniqueness of the ideas in the current context (originality).

In evaluating creative solutions, there are both objective and subjective aspects. Some functional elements, such as the number of added details, are easily evaluated and can be checked off as present or not. Others, such as rating the relative creativity of a given idea, must be done by humans in context.

Creativity is a social construct, meaning society, or the domain or field of study, is often well suited to evaluate what is creative or what isn't. Deciding what is creative and what is more creative is based on our culture and the society in which we live; different societies will have different understandings and acceptance of divergence, originality, and ambiguity. Grading the work within a class or an assignment often requires a form of structure. This is called a rubric, and it is a structured form for evaluating the work.

However, when it comes to evaluating overall creativity, it's often a subjective judgment that relies on the experience and knowledge of others. It weighs the novelty, the applicability, and the expression with current knowledge and experience. In a professional field or domain of knowledge, there are experts who understand the field and who can evaluate the creativity of an effort, and research shows their evaluations are relatively accurate.

There are limits to professional judgment of creativity; managers and those with a vested interest in the field tend to underrate novel ideas because of their own risk aversion or because of habitual criteria. Familiarity does not breed contempt; it builds comfort and an unwillingness to change.

While domain knowledge or expertise is valuable at evaluating creativity, much of the work of the Do Something Different exercises is based on your life experience and your culture. If you have experience with a culture besides your own, you probably have much more to draw on in terms of creative and divergent ideas.

At the same time, our creative efforts in this book are designed to be completed by anyone, building on our "domain" of everyday life. One good way to understand the originality of your efforts is to ask a friend to evaluate your efforts, or, more accurately, you and your friend can complete the same challenge. Research also shows that people who are engaged in comparable creative activities are very accurate in evaluating the creativity of a project. Those who are most accurate at evaluating for the creative nature are people who are creating.

Evaluating the three basic aspects of creativity (originality, applicable, and expressed) can help you develop a broader understanding of your creativity and could provide you with insights as to how to improve.

The nature of what is novel, however, must be subjectively examined as originality and grounded on the reviewers' experience. Based on the rarity or uniqueness of a given solution, here are a few levels of originality:

- The solution is common and has been done a number of times.
- The solution is slightly different from how it's commonly done.
- The solution is infrequent and moderately unusual.
- The solution rarely occurs and might have been done, and it is a significant change from current practice.
- The solution is surprising, unheard of, and not imagined.

Finding ideas or answers that are surprising or unexpected can often elicit laughter, and this is a good indicator of creative output. Comedy is often generated by seeking unusual juxtapositions, new combinations, or inventive propositions. And the work of comics and comedians can be seen as parallel to creative ideas.

One important aspect of being creative is the ability to withhold judgment and to examine new and different ideas. Knowing and expecting a common answer is one thing, but tolerating answers that diverge from the expected is another. We often need to consciously suspend decision making, to purposely reach out for unattractive ideas in our pursuit of the original.

Part of being creative is having tolerance to the unusual and for the ambiguous. This is often contrary to the skills valued in society or in a given field or domain. Pressure to conform with society or in school are often seen as a restraint to creative skill (e.g., Torrance, 1968); managers with a concern for risk also limit creative results (Amabile, 1993). A challenge for creativity is one of acceptance and development of new ideas by a peer group, by a community, or by employers or professional colleagues.

Conclusion

As noted, the evaluation of creativity can have many forms and many aspects, even as it focuses of the individual. Evaluations range from self-reports and short, standard challenges to longer-term evaluations of creative behavior and lifetime accomplishments.

Included this book are a few ways to evaluate your creative potential; this can give you a cursory understanding of your creative skills and a beginning to a broader understanding in seeking to improve your own creativity. Application of your creative skill, generating and improving your ideas must have application to a fuller life, and can also provide you with a better understanding of your capability—for example, if people consistently seek you out for different or good ideas, you may be more creative than the average person. Or if you are consistently looked at as having unusual ideas, it would be a good sign of your creative nature. So with this chapter's Do Something Different, it's important to express your creative output to others and to know that their responses can help you evaluate your own creativity as well.

Do Something Different

Wear something different. Not just the stuff that's in the back of your closet, but rather the stuff that's in your garage, your roommate's closet, your car, or the local hardware store. What can you wear? What limitations do you put on yourself about what you wear? (Only pink? Only cotton? Only store bought? Only clothes? Only Chanel?) Plan it and wear it all day. Record your process and photographs of what you did.

Note that "wearing" means covering some portion of your body and doing it in an observable manner, for an extended period of time. Your change should be noticeable to an ordinary person.

7 | **The Creative Process**

One of the great joys of life is creativity. Information goes in, gets shuffled about, and comes out in new and interesting ways.

—Peter McWilliam

Beyond a Single Creative Act

Opportunities for being creative are integrated in our lives. We have choices to make, tasks to complete, and a life to live, and most of the time we act on these elements without much variance and almost by rote. To encourage our inherent creativity, we must develop a habit of diversity and change: "Cultivating a spirit of everyday nonconformity can foster the development of personality traits and thinking habits that are important to creative achievement. Anything that challenges traditional ways of thinking can also prime the mind for unconventional thinking" (Kaufman & Gregoire, 2015, p. 181).

With some understanding of the process of creativity, we can stretch our capability for exploration and experimentation through the DSDs to any field. We can build our thinking skills through the exercises and learn new methods to help us generate new ideas. We also can increase and store specific and general knowledge and experiences with which to generate new ideas.

In our everyday lives, we need to recognize the choices we make and those we choose not to make. We need to first recognize that these choices can be repetitive and habitual. We can improve these habits to help us

In reality, there is no flash of insight that occurs and no true moment of "eureka!" Ideas develop through a process of learning about the problem, developing an understanding, connecting with your own knowledge and background, and recognizing a larger concept of the challenge (see Sawyer, 2011). Substantial research on insight problems, often using the Remote Associate Test, reveals idea development gradually focusing on an effective solution. This thinking is often not at the conscious level, and that's why insight is often more noticeable.

become more creative: By making more diverse everyday choices, we'll have a greater ability to be creative in our work, in our field of study, and in our larger challenges.

We can build on this insight by learning how to practice and develop our creative skills in our regular lives, and then apply that same capability to our professional problems. For example, we are often asked to solve problems or challenges. Usually, if the problems aren't complex, we solve them by a process we've learned and done over and over. Simple problems are routinely solved, but in many cases the problems are ill-structured. "Real life" also includes a set of challenges that aren't easily defined or understood. These are times when we need to find the things we can do differently and be creative. We need to find the opportunities to see, meet, and explore; to practice the habit of divergent thinking; and to see divergence as a skill.

Iterative, Continuous, and Looping

While a sequential description of how creativity works can describe the similarities of different creative individuals, it's important to remember that being creative and solving problems will involve a number of different ways of working and thinking. Any creative sequence is often iterative, meaning you might go back and find more information or develop a new idea later in the process (Sawyer, 2011; Clinton & Hokanson, 2012). Rigidly following a process and not having this flexibility will decrease your creativity. You can benefit by doing some part of a mental process over or thoroughly shifting your opening idea. Delaying the choice of a final solution can often lead to a more creative answer.

Studies of highly creative designers (Cross, 2006; Lambert & Dorst, 2009) and artists (Sawyer, 2016; Mace & Ward, 2002) show a highly fluid and iterative process of creativity. In most cases, being creative and solving problems is part of artists' or designers' nature and part of the larger ideas and investigations with which they're engaged. Much of the time, individual parts of a "process" are repeated and done outside a regular sequence. To some extent, that's what happens in our own working domain of "real life." We loop, we go back and forth, we do things over, and sometimes we seek alternative results.

Being creative doesn't always follow a set process, as those in various design fields often stray from the parochial processes of their fields, such as architecture or product design. Flexibly changing the process often leads to more appropriate and creative answers (Visscher-Voerman & Gustafson, 2004). Creativity, by definition, necessitates working further from the center of what is commonly accepted.

Understanding

One of the early aspects of the creative process is developing an understanding of the problem or challenge. In many cases the problem is already defined, but often it is ill-structured. There is no specific target or goal, and the ways to solve the problem aren't well known either. There is no objective or perfect answer. Problems that are clear and easily solved are rare.

Essential to finding the problem, to understanding what needs to be done, is an investigation of the nature of the problem itself. This may come from examining the conditions and context, and/or it may build from a long-term understanding of the field.

> All my design life, I've run away from design methods, the cookbook model for solving a problem, perhaps because it forces you to be not very creative. The matter of "*the* creative process" can easily become dogmatic and doctrinaire. Alternatively, if we consider the *way* one is creative, it might illuminate more about how to build creativity into your own life and work.

A lot of creativity starts with an understanding of the current conditions: the domain, the field, the details of what's going on and what has gone on before. For everyday creativity, thinking and knowing the current conditions are important, and bringing in other aspects of our knowledge is equally so. My own initial illustration of fixing my bike tire rested on gathering information from the current location (the drugstore) as well as my background knowledge of fixing a tire. Working as a professional in any field would include knowledge and experience that provides a base for new ideas; being aware of and understanding current conditions would help in terms of both divergent and convergent thinking. However, a creative solution may not come directly from the base knowledge.

Problem Finding

Even when we are given a specific problem to solve, an important aspect of creativity is *problem definition.* In my example of the flat bicycle tire, there were a number of ways to redefine the problem. My problem definition could have been based on the location, needing to get home with my bicycle, or it could have simply been based on not having a bicycle tire repair kit. In the end, it was figuring out a way to keep pressurized air in my bike tire. Finding the right problem to solve is important as well as pragmatic.

Important to our effort for greater creativity is to try different definitions of the problem statement. Restating or redefining the problem is important both in terms of clarity and as a beginning strategy for creativity. By working to clarify or redefine the problem, a different solution may present itself.

Many directions of creative output include the ideas of problem definition and problem finding. New, divergent ideas and answers can spring from redefining a problem and in recognizing the true nature of a problem in the first place. If we want to be more creative, we also need to become more fluid with problem finding. It's not just redefining problems to develop alternative solutions but also identifying problems and seeking a solution. Understanding the initial problem is important; equally important is to understand the "goal" state, or where we ought to be. Somewhere, there needs to be the development of an encompassing approach to the problem, a concept or theme for later ideas.

Synthesis and Concept Development

At some point, you will need to develop a concept, a broader idea about how to address the problem. This may be viewed as redefining the problem or as finding it in the first place. It will develop through your observation, your current focus and beliefs, or some subtle aspect of the challenge that you've noticed.

Some describe this phase as "incubation," but it's not a leisurely phase of unconscious reaction. Rather, it is a synthesis of ideas and research. During the creative process, we must look at the larger issues and ideas and allow the synthesis of what we know and what we've found out. From problem finding and information gathering, we should have a good understanding of the problem and the solution space. We should have an awareness of the larger issues.

Many need some time off task, away from the work on the problem, which is often called "incubation." This will allow the brain to work subconsciously and to find mental resources that might fit. Having time off, either physically or mentally, will aid in finding solutions. Daydreaming, or at least a time to specifically think of the larger issues, is valuable. What we're seeking at this point is synthesis: a broader understanding or reorganization of the challenge, setting a stage for the ideas.

One important aspect is to keep our options open, to not settle for one answer, but to immerse ourselves in the larger set of ideas. This is the synthesis aspect of our creative process.

One thing that I've done that amazes people when we're trying to come up with ideas is to repeatedly re-ask this question: "What are we trying to do here?" This gets us back to our larger goal or clarifies our specific task. It may also get us to explicitly decide what our overall concept is. Restating an understanding of the whole view of a problem helps in refining our insight.

For example, in our first Do Something Different (eat), there were at least three different concepts involved in the challenge of eating something differently. The most apparent one was to eat some substance that you had not eaten before, such as Czech food or endive lettuce or a dollar bill. Another concept for the challenge would be to focus on the manner one eats, and it could include answers such as eating upside-down, underwater, or while standing on one foot. And third, one could develop the concept of different meanings for the word "eat" that don't include food, such as "eat your heart out" (to cause worry), "eat your hat" (to admit a failure of judgment), or "eat your losses" (to take a financial loss), or "eat away my savings" (to use up financial resources). Each is a different concept of how to address the challenge of "eating something different" and represents your synthesis of the idea.

Idea Externalization

A central aspect of creativity is the externalization of ideas; ideas need to leave the brain and be shared or recorded. At the simplest level, this moves the idea from the realm of imagination to the realm of action; we are sharing and exploring our idea by our own actions.

Un-expressed ideas are merely imaginary or fantasy. Expressing ideas is an important aspect of the process of creativity even from the initial stages, when recording nascent ideas is important. Epstein (1996) notes that having a way to record ideas is the simplest way to become more creative. Conceived on waking or when engaged with other activities, new ideas must be recorded or they are easily be forgotten. When ideas are recorded, they can be applied at a later date or combined with others.

Additionally, as the idea is written down or diagramed, it also allows for further improvement of an idea. Our representation of our ideas will let us interact with our own ideas, and it lets us share those ideas with others for their critique, improvement, and adoption. This interaction with your ideas, sometimes called "backtalk," helps you build on the original concepts (Goldschmidt, 2003).

In order to be used, ideas also need to be made public and presented to others for their acceptance and use. Sternberg (2003) describes this as "selling your ideas." This convincing is what moves an idea from being creative to being an innovation; it allows the idea to impact others and to instigate change.

Idea Generation and Combination

Idea generation is not an action that should seek out one workable idea but rather an ongoing aspect of creativity to find more choices and *original* ideas. We need to consciously make the choice to generate more and more ideas. We also should accept the concept that new ideas may not immediately appear workable but could form the basis for transformative change. We need to be aware of the skill of our own generation of ideas, challenging ourselves to continue to come up with different and divergent ideas beyond a single workable idea. These additional ideas can have two benefits; they can be used to check the effectiveness of the first answer, and they can also provide directions for future development.

Having a large number of ideas also opens the opportunity for combinations of ideas, whether for the initial challenge or for future problems. Ideas can be combined to form new ideas and directions.

Evaluation

Throughout the creative process, it is necessary to evaluate our ideas and their expression. Even in the beginning when we are finding problems, we evaluate challenges to undertake or problems that should be solved first. The central tenet of this book, the generation of multiple ideas, still requires evaluation of ideas to select the best, the worst, or the most unusual for further development. The basic argument for evaluation is one of improvement, asking how an idea can be made better. That improvement starts with problem-finding, the synthesis and understanding of the larger issues, idea generation and combination, and elaboration of different aspects of a solution.

Many of the aspects of evaluation are based on our expertise in our field, whether it's nuclear fission or basket weaving. Understanding the context, what has worked in the field, can give us a start at selecting better or more unusual ideas. While extensive knowledge can guide us, without an attitude of risk or experimentation, it will also limit our exploration and the number of our creative ideas.

One of the many clichés that suppress creativity is this: "Why re-invent the wheel?" It's a statement that argues for an existing, workable solution and no change. When seeking creativity, the response could be: "Because we won't get anywhere if we don't change."

The choice to change, to vary, is one of the most important elements of creativity. It is a conscious choice to be creative, to seek more and better answers, and to risk the new in pursuit of the better.

Sometimes this means consciously selecting the idea that is the most challenging and building on that one, knowing it will lead to a different solution. In terms of our earlier creativity exercises, we may know what doesn't work, and we should be evaluating what *could* work.

Another level is to build in the habit of variance, to keep yourself being creative and making divergent choices; you'll then be creative as well as build your knowledge and background for other larger choices.

In summary:

- Beyond a single creative act, creativity must be integrated into our lives.
- Creativity is an iterative process.
- Background knowledge and experience serve as cognitive material for creativity.
- Synthesis and redefinition are a normal part of the process, often called incubation.
- Generating and combining ideas are essential.
- Sharing and externalizing creative ideas improves and validates the answers.

Do Something Different: Give

Plan in advance and implement a gift or giving activity. Document your DSD in writing and through photographs. This should be something you have never done before and/or giving to someone to whom you have never given before. As with other DSDs, the value will come from the activity itself, including its public nature and the ability to impact or connect with others.

8 Techniques for Idea Generation

The hardest ideas to get accepted by others are the brilliant ones, just because they are creative and fly in the face of what everyone else seems to know is true.
— Robert Sternberg and Todd Lubart

There's no magic set of tricks to end up with the single creative answer, whether for an everyday problem or for a defined problem or task at work.

In order to take advantage of our internal skills in addressing challenges, it is helpful to know and be able to use creativity techniques or skills for use. This is the knowledge aspect of our four-part structure of beliefs, habits, skills, and knowledge.

Creative techniques for generating more ideas are common and work in different ways to encourage divergent thinking. As we have seen earlier, we can simply seek more ideas by practicing the production of new ideas, changing attitudes toward new ideas, and developing a habit of generating multiple ideas. We can also build more ideas and more diverse ideas through the use of structures or methods. Some creativity protocols can force diligence in developing ideas as well as encouraging the inclusion of divergent directions. We can learn to move past the limits of our current mental resources, to increase stimulation and experience, and to connect with others by adding new inputs. These include changing habits for learning and seeking challenges and new social and cultural environments. There are a lot of different ways to help you generate more ideas. While it's important to understand various processes, only a few methods are covered in this book. See the "Resources" chapter to a link for a wider range of techniques.

Do methods for idea generation make you more creative, or are such ideas like swim fins: making you swim faster but not a better swimmer? Initially, yes, the ideas outlined here will make you appear to be more creative, but then, with continued practice and internalizing the methods, you will actually be more creative. You will be, to use our metaphor, a better swimmer.

First of all, as we have seen in the previous chapters, we need to train ourselves to generate more possible answers to a challenge. We need to allow more unusual ideas to be considered, suspending our self-censorship and judgment on any given idea before evaluating it. This needs to be internalized as a habit. We need to broaden our active consideration of more diverse ideas.

The methods for generating ideas covered in this chapter were developed through practice in the classroom. Rather than having been designed for simply generating *more ideas*, they are also effective in developing a wider *range* of ideas. They are designed to use unusual stimuli, which often triggers the more divergent ideas we are seeking. The structure these methods provide encourages divergent interactions, moving you past your current mindset and connecting you with other (perhaps more skilled) creatives.

Building on the Alternative Uses Test

From the beginning, we've exercised our creative capacity to generate more ideas from a single starting point. Usually, we begin with an object and simply trying to generate a number of ideas from our own mind and memories. This practice helps us to be more fluid in generating lots of ideas. Along with developing alternative uses for objects, one can also develop alternative scenarios or interpretations of events.

Early research in the field of creativity processes also provide us with some guidelines for this very same exercise. Alex Osborn, an early educator in the field of creativity, developed a checklist of possible answer variations for any alternative uses exercise. These are shown in the Textbox. As we generate ideas to any challenge, we can apply the list, using it to push us to develop more ideas.

Osborn's list included a variety of changes that could be made to a given object or problem. They include the following:

- Adapt to other uses, and apply elsewhere.

- Modify color, sound, smell, sound, meaning, or shape.

- Magnify and add time, height, frequency strength, size, or number. Exaggerate the item.

- Minify through removing anything, making it smaller, lower, shorter, lighter, or left out.

- Substitute with different materials, processes, locations, tone of voice, or personnel.

- Rearrange? Swap components? Alter the pattern, sequence, or layout? Change the pace or schedule? Transpose cause and effect?

- Reverse, do the opposite, go backward, or transpose direction

- Combine units, purposes, or ideas.

Slight modifications could allow even more uses. Simple graphite pencils have been redirected to have different colors, shapes, sizes, and even smells to create a very diverse product group. Changing the scale of an object or product can lead to many other uses; making a tin can smaller opens up many divergent uses such as toys or souvenirs or for specialized uses. Making a brick larger leads to artwork or more-efficient building products.

If different materials are considered for a product, different uses would be possible. For example, while a metal binder clip is pretty simple, making it out of a material that dissolves in the body would make binder clips very useful for internal surgical procedures. Making a brick out of glass changes our understanding of a window as the sole means to get light into a building.

Each of the variations can be applied to any challenge or product and to help us remember to stretch our problem-solving directions. For example, bus problems could be solved by making buses much smaller (providing more detailed service) or by using much larger buses (which could be much more efficient and inexpensive).

Exercise 8.1 Alternative Uses Exercise

Let's try the Alternative Uses Exercise again, but, as you are generating ideas for the given object, try to add at least two responses to each of the verbs listed here: modify, magnify, minify, substitute, rearrange, reverse, and combine. This may help you generate more answers, and it also may help you come up with different types of answers.

Use three minutes to list everything you could do with coins. The coins can be of any size, denomination, or color, and you can use as many as you wish and of any size you wish. Come up with as many ideas as you can. There are no wrong answers, but try and include divergent ideas for each modifier.

Figure 8.1 Alternative Uses Exercise: Coins

Magnify (Make Larger)

1. _____

2. _____

3. _____

Minify (Make Smaller)

4. _____

5. _____

6. _____

Substitute (Change Aspects of Coins)

7. _____

8. _____

9. _____

Reverse

10. _____

11. _____

12. _____,

Combine

13. _____

14. _____

15. _____

This capability can be increased in everyone through practice, but it is limited due to the simple, single starting point. We might have good ideas hidden in our brains that are not easily accessed. However, research by Epstein (1996) and others on both human and animal subjects has shown that supposedly inadvertent, open-ended hints, like random words or pictures, can trigger new ideas that did not immediately come to mind when faced with a challenge.

Mindmaps

Most of the time we've worked with a linear list of verbal ideas, and, when we begin to work with different viewpoints or conceptual areas, it's effective to work in two dimensions, mapping out an idea and different directions.

This is a good method to lay out all of your ideas and associations with a topic in a visual manner. You're free to make connections you may not have thought of before. Essentially, mindmaps are a way of describing divergent directions in a visual manner. And to help trigger new ideas much in the way, the simple act of doodling or drawing allows your mind to think more clearly and creatively. One way to evaluate the inherent creativity in a mindmap is to count the number of directions that are investigated, which examines *flexibility*, and to count the details that are added on to each branch of the mindmap, which illustrates *elaboration*. These are two concepts for evaluating creativity that were discussed in Chapter 3.

At their core, mindmaps utilize existing knowledge and allow you to make connections by free association or laying out ideas in a non-linear structure. Information is visually categorized and structured to create some type of hierarchy. You have more freedom to find connections to other ideas as your map grows.

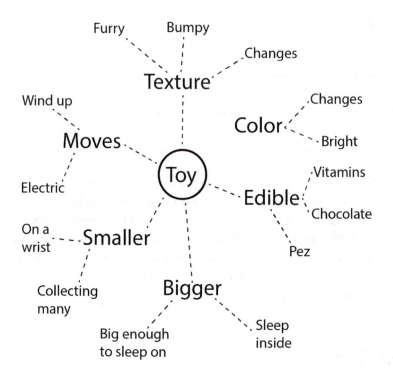

Figure 8.2 A mindmap starting from the word "toy" to generate new ideas for toys; first-level changes are drawn from Osborne's list.

They are a convenient way for anyone, visual thinkers in particular, to jot down notes or generate ideas as quickly and with freedom from self-censoring of ideas. In addition, free mindmapping software exists that can help with the visual and spatial organization of information. And you'll find the link to that in the "Resources" chapter.

Beyond generating interesting ideas, another useful thing with mind-maps is that they are a good way to organize information with graphic elements, such as color, shape, or size for emphasis. Or to make connections between the subcategories later on.

Trying to define an abstract concept can sometimes be difficult, but it helps to take advantage of the visual format of mindmaps. When you want to connect one idea to another in a different category on the other side of the web, you can use a certain element like color or shape to make that connection.

While changing the way we manipulate an object to generate more ideas, we can also change our viewpoint in addressing a problem or generating ideas by using mindmaps.

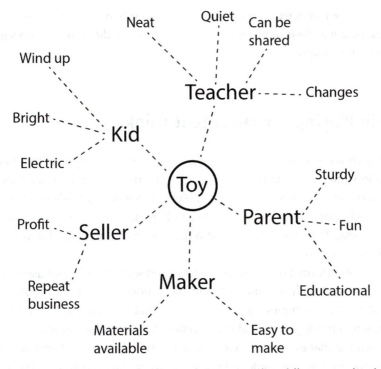

Figure 8.3 The starting points for the mindmap now utilize different people who
have an interest in toys. Each one generates a different set of ideas and
directions.

Another way we can generate new ideas and new alternative uses is to
assume different roles or view the challenge from different directions. So
this time, let's imagine a child's toy (of your choice) with the goal to make
the toy "better." Let's use the different roles that connect with a toy to generate new ideas. Each toy has as an end-user, a child. Most of the time, connected with the child and with the toy are parents, teachers, toy makers,
the toy seller, and other interested parties. Each of these will have different
ideas and viewpoints as to what would make the toy better. The manufac-
turer would like to make the toy more easily and may make changes to the
toy for that purpose; some of these will be to the benefit of the child, and
others won't. The seller would like to make as much money as possible
selling the toy, which may mean that fewer parents and children are able
to buy the toy. The specific changes each party would make would vary
with their own expertise. We all have the most familiarity with the role of
the child and could imagine a great range of different changes in the toy

based on our own experience. We can imagine how each of the different roles, acting in their own interests, would argue for different elements in a revised toy design.

Role Playing for Divergent Thinking

Research has shown that imaginary play and role playing as a child helps develop creative capabilities, which are carried forward to adulthood. Additionally, a good way to solve problems and investigate ideas is to role-play with more complex problems (Van Hoorn, et al., 1993). One model for bringing forth different ideas is a famous creativity method developed by Edward DeBono.

DeBono's method uses six hats to represent six different aspects of thinking, and each is represented in discussion or solving a problem. A white hat that examines the facts, a red hat that expresses and works from emotion, a black judgmental hat, a yellow hat that is logical and positive, a green hat that expresses creativity, and a blue hat focused on overview and process. If we examine the toy again, we'll end up with a different set of answers and ideas from each area of responsibility. For example, toys may be redesigned to help express emotion or creativity, or they may be examined as part of a larger understanding of play. Dividing the world into cognitive direction can help lead us to a wider set of answers, and hope-fully to better answers.

This also leads to a more open and undirected way of seeking different orientations on the solution of any given problem or explanation: the Oneida Rule of Six. This method recognizes the wide range of possible explanations for any solution or experience and, as an ongoing habit, encourages the development of divergent ideas.

> The Rule of Six says that for each apparent phenomenon, devise at least six plausible explanations, every one of which can indeed explain the phenomenon. There are probably sixty, but if you devise six, this will sensitize you to how many there may yet be and prevent you from locking in on the first thing that sounds right as The Truth.
>
> (Underwood Spencer, 1990, p. 19)

How we can use this in our pursuit of being more creative should be clear. We understand that the initial answer is often not creative and that we must seek additional answers or options. Finding the other "plausible" alternatives is, by definition, creative. This Native American tradition uses one's location in the world to find answers: looking to the front, back, above, below, left, and right; each perspective should help you develop a different answer.

The Native American tradition, like DeBono's Thinking Hats, encourages us to examine different viewpoints and ideas and to provide a structure for generating ideas. Both methods remind us to go beyond our own simple understanding and beyond our safe and uncreative first answer.

Attribute Listing

Attribute listing is another very effective way of generating new ideas. Usually, it begins from observations about an object or a system. The object I often use as a focus is a refrigerator as they are relatively common and as my own refrigerator shares its attributes with millions of other refrigerators. Attributes are properties of an object or system. The important starting point is to list as many of the attributes as are possible as each aspect can be improved or changed.

We'll walk through making a list of things that describes a refrigerator.

What properties define a refrigerator? First of all, it tends to be boxy. It tends to be white, or it could be black, or it could be stainless steel. Sometimes they're other colors. A lot of times the refrigerator has two inside areas, and one of them (the freezer) is cold, and the other, the main area of the refrigerator, is cool.

Often, refrigerators have a flat top, and sometimes a cat goes up there, and sometimes people put things like cereal boxes up there. A lot of times they have a dusty thing on the bottom, where it sucks in air for cooling. And, most of the time, they're powered by electricity. The outside surface can have magnets on it. People also put art up either on the front or the sides, not on the back because that's usually against the wall. They're often in the kitchen, and, aside from that, it also hums some of the time, probably because it doesn't know the words.

Attribute Listing a Refrigerator

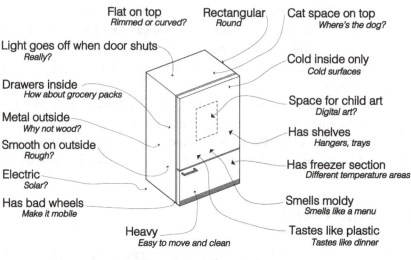

Flat on top
Rimmed or curved?

Rectangular
Round

Cat space on top
Where's the dog?

Light goes off when door shuts
Really?

Drawers inside
How about grocery packs

Metal outside
Why not wood?

Smooth on outside
Rough?

Electric
Solar?

Has bad wheels
Make it mobile

Heavy
Easy to move and clean

Cold inside only
Cold surfaces

Space for child art
Digital art?

Has shelves
Hangers, trays

Has freezer section
Different temperature areas

Smells moldy
Smells like a menu

Tastes like plastic
Tastes like dinner

Figure 8.4 Attribute Listing

One important way to develop your attribute list is to go beyond your memory and your visual observations and to perceive a refrigerator through your other senses; for example, imagine (or discover) what or how a refrigerator *tastes*. We usually don't taste our refrigerators, nor do we pay attention to the smell, unless you do that by accident when you open the door. (And then it's usually bad.)

The next step is to change each of those things you listed that could provide us with an idea for a future product. Again, we need to be open and accepting of unusual ideas. So, one thing we could do is try to make a round refrigerator. We would have to put it someplace else, not in the corner or on the side of the room. Or we can have a number of different places at various cooling temperatures inside the new refrigerator. Instead of cool, we'll make it variable. And it could be red, or it could be pink, or it could be made out of wood. All of these are possible. And this is a great way for people to develop new products.

We could also have six different temperature zones in the refrigerator. Instead of a freezer on the bottom, we could just skip the freezer altogether, or we can have multiple freezers: the deep freezer area, and a slightly warmer one that doesn't chill your ice cream too much. So, maybe we'll have two freezers.

We can also try to do something about the dustiness. We know a refrigerator is going to attract cat hair, dirt, and lint, so maybe we accept that as a given and add an air filter on the bottom of our refrigerator that we can clean often. The refrigerator could help keep the house clean by purposely collecting dirt from the house.

Refrigerators do not have to be electrically powered either, at least not tied to the regular power grid. In a sunny climate it would make sense to have a solar powered refrigerator, like a solar powered air conditioner. When the sun shines it could power the refrigerator given enough solar panels. The power consumption would be tied to the power generation. A refrigerator could also be cooled by cold water or through ammonia gas as a refrigerant. This means you could move it out of the kitchen, out of the house, and into the back yard. How different!

Trying It Yourself

3M's Post-it Notes is a great example of how changing attributes can generate new product ideas. It was a single, simple product that has developed into a diverse family of products. When they were first sold, they were small, unlined, light-yellow paper squares in a stack and somewhat sticky—and that's our first listing of attributes. Each of these attributes can be changed to generate new product ideas that we may have seen:

Small: Size ranges from very small, 2 cm × 3 cm to poster size to wall size.

Unlined: Various designs are now printed in various colors.

Yellow: Beyond pastels, they are available in bright intense colors and black.

Square: Post-Its are now produced in rectangular shapes as well as various novelty shapes such as hearts or clover leafs.

Creating a mindmap can be a good way to do the attribute listing exercise; the illustration above is a form of a mindmap. In this case, Post-It notes are the subject and the product we're looking to alter. And so that becomes the central idea, with the second level of nodes being the traits to be altered. And how could each of them change? From here, you can list which traits can be changed and organize each subcategory easily. So again, jot down different ways you can change the shape or material of a Post-it to give it a new use.

Exercise 8.2 Mindmapping Exercise

Draw your own mindmap using the square as a representation of a Post-it Note. In this case, Post-it Notes are the subject and the product we're looking to alter. That becomes the central idea, with the next level of nodes being the attributes that could be altered. Then imagine how each of them could change. From here, you can list which traits can be changed and organize each subcategory easily. So again, jot down different ways you can change the shape or material of a Post-it to give it a new use.

In this case, creating a Post-it out of a different material, like fabric, would allow you to make visual associations to new uses of the product. Also, thinking about different ways traits can be changed. For example, oversized Post-its made from fabric could have a use in apparel.

While some ideas may be odd, or may not seem to be practical, the idea is that you're free to write down whatever comes to mind, even if it doesn't make any sense at the time.

The trick with attribute listing is to be very complete and then in extreme detail when you list attributes. And you can do this with a process as well as with an object. More extensive lists of attributes are more effective at generating possibilities for new ideas.

And then, go through and develop a possible change for each attribute. You can make Post-it Notes better. You can make them worse. You can make them bigger or smaller, but you've got your list of prompts in terms of what you can change to make your object completely different.

Changes that result from attribute listing (and comparable processes) are small and don't significantly redirect the product concept. While we can change the details of a refrigerator or Post-it Note, we probably don't think of changing the central concept of a refrigerator, to preserve food by keeping it cold, or the central concept of a Post-it note, an adhesive-backed writing material that sticks anywhere. Transformational change, great change, occurs when conceptual change is undertaken. Imagine a food preservation machine that kept food at room temperature or Post-it Notes that let go from their location after a certain period of time.

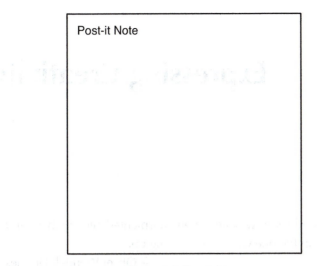

Figure 8.5 Post-it Note

How we use these methods and others can help us build our personal capability for creativity. But to effectively express our ideas and get them accepted, we will need to reach outside for more inspiration and collaboration with our peers. Those will be covered in the following chapters.

DSD: Talk to Someone Different

One of the challenges in developing creativity and building your own experiences is to stretch the collection of people with whom you interact. Usually we talk to the same people every day, and that number of people is relatively small. This "different" is designed to broaden your experiences and continue the development of your creativity skills.

You are to talk to someone with whom you would not ordinarily speak. The process is to develop ideas for three different creative people with which to talk, select one and plan in advance how you will contact and engage with that person. It is important that **you do this in person** and not via any media: i.e., no telephone, email, chat, video, cell phone, or other communication technology. Ask them at least five open-ended questions. The goal is to stretch your own set of human interactions, and enjoy the events of your conversation. Save the experience through photographs and your notes.

9 | **Expressing Creativity**

Many ideas grow better when transplanted into another mind than in the one where they sprang up.

—Oliver Wendell Holmes

While our beginning definition of creativity focused on ideas that are "original and worthwhile" or "new and useful," externalizing our ideas is also an essential aspect of the creative process. Expressing our ideas moves our thoughts past imagination, toward action and implementation. Drawing, writing, proclaiming, and sharing our ideas can help us generate more ideas, can help us improve our concepts, and allows us become more capable of bringing thoughts to fruition.

We get much value from expressing ideas when we are able to capture the results of our thinking and our imagination. Articulating and recording of ideas is worthwhile as it helps us retain and remember our ideas. This allows their improvement through our editing and revision; we then have the ability to examine, to edit, and to improve our ideas. Expression of our ideas also allows us to share with others and to receive their comments, to build on their observations, and hopefully to successfully collaborate.

Saving Ideas

Many ideas begin when our logical, orderly mind is not as controlling, "where attention is defocused, when thought is associative, and when a large number of mental representations are simultaneously activated" (Martindale, 1999). This condition of openness, when one is relaxed, day-dreaming, or half awake, can also occur through practice, but recording the ideas then developed is critical. Ideas in the mind are fragile and capricious; they come and go, and if they're not recorded or captured they may be lost.

> While creative people are diligent about recording their ideas, often they set aside a specific time for thinking divergently and allowing ideas to develop. Having a designated time for free-thinking . . . daydreaming . . . will help newer ideas reach the forefront. Spending regular times on your thinking will help in most forms of creativity, whether convergent or divergent. Specific locations may be helpful as well; a space away from the action and ongoing flow of ordinary tasks will let thoughts develop.

Most creative people have some way of capturing their ideas *at any time* to avoid losing them. Artists and designers habitually record and develop their ideas through sketching or drawing in notebooks or journals. We still are amazed at the creativity expressed in Leonardo Da Vinci's notebooks. The notebooks are more than just visually pleasing and interesting images. They allowed for the development of his thoughts, and the sharing of his ideas with others.

There is an old cliché about inventors' great ideas often being developed on the backs of napkins; there is some truth to this. In general, simple methods are best for spontaneous ideas. Whatever material is at hand is often put to use. For example, graphic designer Milton Glaser developed and sketched the initial version of the I Love NY logo on a scrap piece of paper in the back of a taxi (Lehrer, 2012). It is critical to capture fleeting ideas when they occur, whether in bed, in the shower, or at other times.

Building Complex Ideas

We also know ideas do not usually arise fully formed from one's mind. Unique combinations and concepts take a while to develop, and addressing details and challenges requires revision and interaction. Complex ideas are multifaceted and include a range of scale and detail. For these aspects of the process, it's necessary to record and develop the various elements separately, later relating to the whole.

The other main benefit of externalizing ideas is that it allows you to be able to evaluate your own work. Writing, painting, and composing all present ideas in an external form, and, in each, the authors/creators are able to see and interact with their ideas. Goldschmidt (2003) called this the "backtalk of sketching"; trying different components of complex ideas, judging them, and improving them. Sketching, visually or verbally, can be described as distributed cognition, thinking both inside and outside the brain. We can see, improve, and re-arrange different parts of the idea, whether it is a verbal representation (as in writing this book), or in a musical composition, or in the layout of a building.

Diversifying Idea Input

This external aspect of the creative process also allows sharing and interaction with others about our ideas. Ideas in the open, in the public realm, can be improved, increased, combined, or challenged. Expression allows ideas to be shared with others, just like our own ability to review and improve our own ideas when they are made visible.

While this book focuses on the development of individual creative capability, we also need to understand that "[much] creativity emerges from complex social and organizational systems" (Sawyer, 2011, p. 419). In other words, sharing and engaging with other people helps develop creative ideas and will take you beyond where you can reach by yourself.

Our ideas originate from our own experience and knowledge. Necessarily, that is limited to the contents of our own mind, to our own memories and knowledge. Our ideas take form from internally combining ideas and processes. While we can build our experiences over the long run, including others in a discussion of our work quickly adds their understanding and possible ideas. Working with other people, either through conversation or collaborative effort, encourages the development of different ideas. Research has shown interaction and discussion with others helps develop more creative and better ideas (Sawyer, 2011).

The first benefit of talking with others is a way of building on their experiences and is similar to exploring new environments. The ideas, histories, and actions of others can all lead to different input for your creative ideas. As we've seen, creativity builds from diverse input and stimuli; more experiences and interactions provide a broader base for creative thinking, more bricks from which to build concepts. Pragmatically, we talk to other people because they have seen and done things we haven't, and this can help make our ideas better.

Imagine the capability of doubling or tripling your own memories to use in improving your ideas. Sharing your work with others allows their experience and knowledge to inform the work. This adds to our original ideas through a diversity of input; explaining and building on questions from colleagues, peers, and friends.

One thing that often concerns people is losing control of their idea. A brilliant idea might be stolen or misdirected. While the control of intellectual property is important, it's more critical to be able to develop and advance your idea by working with other people. The media often portrays the act of creation as an extremely individual act, accomplished alone, and through sheer brilliance. In most cases, however, the advancement of an idea does involve outside influences, and, for an idea to be accepted, it needs to be made public (Johnson, 2010).

Critique

Research does say that our own evaluation of our creative ideas is generally over-positive. We're proud of our ideas and think they're great, but we need to use outside evaluation to honestly understand their quality. Their experience, their domain knowledge, will play a role in their evaluation of your ideas. Review of your ideas by others can help you check your logic and see other possibilities for your ideas.

The challenge in sharing your work is how to organize your efforts to get the most of the connections and interactions you have. Creativity often comes from outside inputs, from external stimuli as we've seen, and, similarly, the ideas of others can help improve your ideas and your work (Epstein, 1996). Colleagues, friends, and peers will all ask questions about your ideas; the questions they ask may not have occurred to you, or you might have addressed them already. In any case, the more well-thought out questions regarding your potential idea, the better the result from your effort.

In the design fields, there's a history of showing your work to others for their comments and observations. Designers and architects learn early on to engage others in discussions about their ideas. It's generally called a critique. Similarly, writers often have other people read their work: poems, books, or stories. And those in the scientific fields generally circulate their research papers to colleagues for comment before the writing is sent for review and publication. The goal is to improve the ideas through review by trusted and honest colleagues.

Beyond the simple interaction of critiquing and sharing ideas with others, the value of sharing is complex. It ranges from social support to adoption of ideas by others (actual innovation).

Sharing the work also helps us develop a social contract to *be creative*. Others' recognition of our creative acts and the expectation of our creativity will drive us to be even more creative.

Our ideas also must be effectively shared for them to be of value or to be accepted by others. The acceptance of new ideas requires what Sternberg (2003) calls "selling your ideas." Because your idea, if novel, might be very different than the results expected by others, it will still need to be explained and demonstrated.

Context

We also all need to be creative in our social context. What is creative in the United States may be old hat in Europe; some things you can do any day in Cambodia could be considered highly unusual in the West. One example of this occurred in one of my online classes, where a student from Cambodia regularly ate tarantulas as a high-protein snack, but for her DSD (eat), she put them on a sandwich, which she had never done before.

We often view the outside world as a constraint, a limitation on what we can do or achieve. In some areas, we have free rein and are able make our own unusual and expressive choices; in others, we are limited by our context. And then there are some areas in which we limit ourselves and make creatively smaller choices.

What an artist does normally may be completely out of bounds in the corporate world, and vice versa. We can begin with smaller actions toward creativity, building a reputation for creativity, and with a goal of being more substantial in our creative results, adjusted to our context.

From the earliest days of research and theory in creativity, to newer concepts of group collaboration, improvisation, and acceptance, it's clear that creative ideas need to be expressed and shared. When we can see and edit our ideas in some form, we can make them better. And when we share these ideas, the comments, critiques, and responses all help improve our concepts. This is especially true with more extensive collaborative efforts, included in the following.

Creative Collaboration

There are historical examples of collaboration and idea development, from single ideas to societal development. Steven Johnson, writing in *Where Good Ideas Come From* (2010), highlights the coffee house as the public venue that spurred the industrial revolution in England. Stimulated by caffeine, people would meet and discuss ideas, develop projects, and interact with each other. There's evidence that the close working of Wilbur and Orville Wright gave them the capability to create powered flight before their competitors (Sawyer, 2011; Castells, 2014).

It also happens in technological development as exemplified by the legendary developments in Silicon Valley. In fact, it's generally known that Silicon Valley developed faster than other areas due to a culture of sharing and interaction where gathering spots like the Wagon Wheel, a Silicon Valley bar, encouraged interaction and sharing of ideas (Castells, 2014). Much of the success of Apple, Facebook, Google, and other major corporations comes from a continuing series of intermingled interactions and collaboration. Similarly, the premise of academic publishing is to build on the ideas of others; collaborative, competitive, and open research on major innovations supports the engagement with others in developing ideas (Johnson, 2010).

Ideas often flourish in a rich, fluid environment, and building that environment inside an organization is a challenge. It occurs with good jazz groups as well as productive research labs. It happens in the art world, for example, as it did with the strong interactions of the original Impressionists.

Many people hesitate to share or reveal their ideas to others. However, the benefits of collaboration and critique are substantial. Accurate comments can help you avoid glaring errors and could enhance your work. Sharing also allows you to see if you're representing your idea well, helps you with details of the idea, and allows you to see if you're meeting your creative goal. Acceptance of your idea, that is, innovation, relies on the acceptance of your ideas by others.

Interaction

One of the best examples of a trusting and yet creative environment comes from the field of improv comedy. Improv is an unscripted performance form that relies on interaction between participants.

Improv artists or actors often employ a rule when working with others called "yes, and . . . ," where all new directions and ideas are accepted and built upon. It is a challenge and a capability that is most valuable. The idea builds on accepting a given premise for a skit, such as driving a bus, and then adds to that initial idea, advancing the story line. The story could involve doing things while driving the bus, actions of the riders of the bus, or what happens to the bus, but each idea is accepted as a new starting point.

Using this process is also possible in the development of an idea. The beginning premise, *yes*, is accepted, *and* subsequent additive ideas are added. These ideas are helpful, building on the original idea and moving it forward.

Of course, this requires others who are both appropriately skilled and capable of working with someone else's idea. Unfortunately, many times people offer negative criticism right off the bat, without an accompanying positive or constructive set of ideas. It is important to develop your own network of people that can help you move your idea forward, whether by honest criticism or by inventive possibilities.

In reality, we usually have a social network that supports us in class or at work. We discuss how we did on a test, complain about homework levels, and see how someone else did on the latest project. From those interactions, we can build a network of colleagues and groups with which to work. They're in place, self-selected, and moderately efficient at completing tasks.

How this starts is with your own reaction or critique of ideas, your own use of "yes, and . . ." when people share their ideas with you. Consciously using that structure in working with others is crucial at first, and eventually it becomes part of your interactive process. You can learn from others' ideas as well, with their divergent backgrounds and different thinking methods. And you'll be better at your work by critiquing *their* ideas.

Exercise 9.1: A Three-Line Scene

Aside from taking an improv class, there are some things you can do to increase your interactions with others. Let's practice some interaction with off-the-cuff conversational ideas.

To start, you'll need someone else to work with as this is a collaborative activity. Begin by explaining to the person the concept of responding positively to statements, and the use of "yes, and. . ."

In the scene, the first person makes a point of view statement from real life, beginning with "I want . . . ," "I feel . . . ," or "I am . . ." Then the other person, accepting the first statement, builds on it and answers beginning with "Yes, and . . ." followed by a comment. Then the first person finishes with a "discovery" line.

Here's an example:

Person 1: I feel tired.
Person 2: Yes, and you haven't slept for eight days.
Person 1: I guess I shouldn't be working at Starbucks and drinking all that coffee.

Reverse the roles and continue trying this exercise for three rounds, switching roles every round.

The next step would be to try this new skill of "Yes, and . . ." in a general conversation, building ideas and moving a discussion forward. While it doesn't directly develop new ideas, it builds an ability to comment and interact with other people and with ideas. Also, it builds our capability for elaboration, one of the metrics of creativity.

Exercise 9.2: Consequences Problem

We should also re-visit an earlier exercise that focused on adding details to our initial ideas. This time, we can use a partner to build more onto our ideas. This simple means of structured collaboration can provide a good model for integration in an ongoing manner.

This exercise also should be done with a partner. The challenge is similar to the creativity evaluation in the first section of the book. This time, however, both of you will respond to the first question, but the other person will add the details. You should share your ideas when done, as well as the elaboration you've made with your partner's concepts.

Let's imagine you came home one day and learned your neighbor had just won the lottery. What would be the *disadvantages* of this? What could be the negative consequences of this event? Use three minutes to generate as many bad outcomes for this event as possible. Don't limit your answers; write as many possible answers as you can.

Once you've used the entire time coming up with possible disadvantages to the situation, exchange idea lists, and spend five more minutes adding multiple details to each other's answers. Share your answers and see how they are similar and different. Like the other exercises, this is about learning a creative thinking technique as well as practicing creativity.

Working in Teams

This book has a Western orientation to the work and is focused on personal or individual creativity, and it is directed toward products or results. The generation of new ideas is viewed mainly as an individual event. Other cultures may view *individual* creativity as less desirable and would support a more community-based model for creativity (Kim, 2007). At the same time, working in a modern society and recognizing the value of collaboration, group or team efforts are also necessary. While there are great advantages to working with others in terms of generating more ideas and critiquing your work, working with others in an individualistic society is often challenging.

For example, when we're in school, many group projects aren't successful, and we think we could do the work more efficiently by ourselves. The same also occurs at work. There are difficult engagements with others, with social loafing of group members, and with disagreements about ideas are often poorly resolved.

So how do you make a group work better together?

This book is less focused on explanations of how groups work and more on encouraging creative results from both personal and group efforts. Successful team efforts often begin with having an appropriate selection of participants and a good process in place for the work. Unfortunately, many times groups are formed for reasons that aren't always in the best interests of creativity. These groups, composed of friends, colleagues, and social connections often share the same ideas and backgrounds, and they aren't that helpful for being divergent or creating novel ideas. They're great for feedback and working together, but not for coming up with something new. Why should they be? They have the same environment and background and probably the same ideas, and they want to maintain their social connections as well. For creativity, it's important to include those with different backgrounds and ideas, with different capabilities and interests. In short, homogenous groups are good at getting things done; heterogeneous groups are able to develop more divergent responses to challenges, and this guideline is accurate both in school and at work.

Understanding expectations for process and outcome is generally helpful in avoiding teamwork problems. Using specific processes of idea generation can help increase group interaction and can also be used to encourage a wider range of inputs.

We all need to find others to help make our creativity better—not only those that give good support, but others that add more diversity to the process. And when we're professionally advanced, we will need to find ways to spur deep thinking and more divergent efforts.

Brainstorming

One good way to work with a group is through a set of practices called "brainstorming." It's a term that a lot of people use indiscriminately to describe an unorganized group session where everyone comes up with different ideas at once. That's a good beginning, but the brainstorming process, developed by Alex Osborn in the 1950s, has a little more structure and encourages all to participate and to accept others' ideas for consideration (Osborn, 1963). The brainstorming process builds on the deferral of judgment, an important characteristic of creativity; it allows us to go past the first workable idea to explore other divergent and original options. Osborn also recognized that the form and structure of brainstorming would vary with the situation, with no set way to brainstorm.

Some Basic Rules Are:

1. Avoid the evaluation of ideas, as this tends to restrict discussion and idea generation. Ideas from each participant need to be included in the discussion.

2. An open and freewheeling atmosphere will encourage a broader range of ideas. The wilder the ideas, the better.

3. Having a greater quantity of ideas will increase the number of original ideas generated, as it does when working as an individual.

4. Building on the previous ideas of others is critical, as combination and improvement will follow.

Groups for brainstorming can be of varied sizes, although larger groups tend to decrease the number of original or usable ideas. Group sizes of three to five are effective, and they can be as large as eight (Osborn, 1963; Chaffin, 1985; Coyne & Coyne, 2011). If groups are too large, productivity loss occurs when people need to wait for their time to speak or comment. Larger groups often need a designated recorder or facilitator to keep the process organized. This facilitator can keep the process on track even for small groups.

A clear goal for brainstorming sessions will encourage more ideas and better performance. Building on a single charge or task is important. Simpler tasks are better for inexperienced brainstormers.

Each participant, in turn, describes an idea for the topic. Going around the group in order ensures complete participation. Others in the group can add to any idea, but not criticize or praise the idea. Or, they can begin anew with their own idea.

After a set period of time, such as 15–20 minutes, idea generation should stop. After this phase, the group should select the better ideas in discussion. Generally, groups are much better at choosing the best ideas than are individuals.

While this is a well-regarded method in the popular mind, there are ways to get more out of the system (Lehrer, 2012; Paulus, 1999; Larey & Paulus, 1999). For example, it's generally better to have the participants individually generate a written list of ideas before starting the group conversation (McMahon, et al. 2016). Generating and recording ideas beforehand will provide a base of ideas with which to work. This form of individual idea production may double the available ideas. The writing of ideas can be used either as a mental start to the exercise or as a list for each participant to voice in turn. It also helps more introverted participants to offer ideas. A variation is for ideas to be posted using Post-it Notes, with group members walking around to read and improve the various ideas.

There are a couple of creative limits to brainstorming groups and group work in general. Group members tend to get focused or fixated on a single idea or type of idea. Participants with valuable ideas can be inhibited by the group setting or dynamics. And some group members may not feel as responsible, due to what is called "social loafing." With awareness, all can be avoided to some extent.

Using the brain's storming process can give you insight as to how groups can generate more ideas. Seeing how others are creative can also help us understand our own ideas better as well.

Exercise 9.3

Try using a structured brainstorming process with your own group of friends or family: start with a simple goal, such as figuring out what to do for dinner or what to do for fun on a week night. Have each participant write down some ideas on a 3×5 card or piece of paper. Encourage each to be original in their ideas and tell them to the group.

The overall goal is to generate a lot of ideas. Each new idea could be elaborated through additions from other group members. In a brainstorming group, applying the "yes, and. . ." model can help build on ideas after the initial round of idea production. Conclude the process by reviewing the ideas and selecting the better ideas for implementation.

Talking to Creatives

After we understand the value of sharing and collaborating, we can extend that idea to proactively meeting with and engaging new people who are creative. While we can learn from many other people as to how they are creative, those people who are exceptionally creative may be able to give us methods and ideas as to how to make ourselves be more creative.

Can you find creativity in everyday life? Some other people do demonstrate a high level of creativity, but often aren't recognized for being creative as an artist, designer, or performer. We know, also, that some people are *more* creative, that they are known for their ability to develop new ideas and create new things. We can apply the same standards with which we began; we are looking for those people with new approaches to challenges and that are appropriate and useful.

For example, I know from experience that hardware stores' need to be responsive and inventive goes beyond the ability to mentally catalog where everything is in their store. This extends to the ability to solve poorly defined, complex problems. I recently had an experience at a hardware store that illustrated the creative and problem-solving capacity of their staff.

My wife and I went to a hardware store, and she was seeking weights to make a dress design properly drape or hang. After hearing the problem and offering one solution, the store clerk went through a number of other possible solutions by presenting each of them throughout the store. The problem was small, but had some complexity and had no obvious solution. While the first answer, lead sinkers for fishing, was workable and inexpensive, we also examined a range of other possible solutions before selecting a few to try out. The staff in a hardware store is charged with addressing the varied problems of customers. The problems may not be well stated or described, and quite often the solution is not evident in any single piece of hardware. Creativity is demonstrated by helping provide possible solutions to a wide range of clients.

We know many think of creativity as being resident in famous people, in the arts, the sciences, or the humanities. This can be described as "big C" creativity, which is the creativity of the famous, who have, through their work, changed their fields. These are people who are creative on a national or an international level, such as Picasso, Einstein, Shakespeare, and Hawking. Some believe creativity can be best understood by examining those who are creative (see, for example, Csikszentmihalyi, 1996).

In the class on which this book is based, I ask each student to interview their other faculty members and ask them about their own creativity. They learn much from those meetings, and they see how creativity is used in many fields to develop new ideas and direction for work.

However, this excludes the many people who are creative on a more local level and who are working professionals in various fields. This level of creativity is rooted in solving problems, generating original work, and dealing with others as a regular aspect of a profession. This can be called "pro C" (or "professional") creativity (Kaufman & Beghetto, 2009).

For example, at a university, each of the faculty is charged with being creative through their research and their writing as well as through their innovative practices in the classroom. They try new models of the work and solve different, new problems every day. To some extent, we should all seek to reach this level as a step beyond our everyday scope of creativity.

The writing in this book focuses on the creativity we engage in on an everyday basis, the creativity of our lives, which is referred to as "little c" creativity. We are seeking to build our creativity in our everyday lives, which can be extended to our more professional activities whether that is art or accounting. But one very most accessible aspect of higher creativity is by connecting to those in careers or occupations who are necessarily creative. Examining the practice of the creative professional or the highly creative individual has value for us who are developing our everyday creativity. It can help you better understand your own creativity, and you can learn from them aspects of the process and maintenance of a high state of creativity.

While personally discussing with local creatives can help us understand creativity at a professional level, this exercise can help us develop our own everyday creativity, by giving us more accessible models for being creative. The value of talking to others about their creativity is that we may be able to distill some of their traits for ourselves.

Do Something Different: Meeting Creatives

Here, you are being asked to be more of an observer, separate from your own being creative, and to see how others have maintained and improved their own creative efforts. What one should notice about talking with creatives is their ability to connect ideas and thoughts with their own work. How do they maintain their creativity or keep their ideas fresh?

The first step is to find people who are creative and are willing to talk about their process. They should be known for generating multiple and usual ideas, but those that are still appropriate to the context. They may be known for ideas that help them solve unusual and complex problems. They solve problems when no one else can, not so much by their knowledge, but for their inventiveness. You may know of such creative people, or they can be found by asking others for their recommendations.

They may not define themselves as being creative; they may have observed they have a lot of ideas, ideas that are unusual. They are often curious and probably have a sense of humor; they have met challenges and failure, and persisted.

The questions you will need to ask must go beyond the factual and should seek to develop an understanding of their practices and work. The creativity of their lives may not be tied to specific products but will be found more in their habits and practices. A goal your questioning is to get them to discuss the more subtle aspects of their lives. Here are some questions that could be worthwhile:

Could you tell me about some time you solved a problem for someone?

How is the way that you work different from others in your field?

Could you tell me about a time you were stuck on a particular challenge?

Could you describe any habits you have that help you discover solutions or new directions?

You will need to vary the questions to fit whom you're talking to and your own talking style, and to be respectful of their time and efforts.

Any person can be creative in their area of activity. How they are creative, and the appropriateness of their creativity varies, but they demonstrate the ability to generate alternative answers and to be open to other interpretations.

Why talk with them? You should be able to develop insights as to how to better be creative, see the divergent methods of staying creative, and begin to understand actual experiences in being creative. Write down or record their responses; photograph, with permission, their working spaces, and review the material at a later time.

Imagine talking with a mechanic. The mechanic's goal is to diagnose what is wrong with a car and solve it. Sometimes the mechanic figures out the right answer, sometimes the wrong answer, and sometimes he or she is stuck. The mechanic has a base of knowledge, but also ways of working, thinking, and exploring challenges. The mechanic's ability to resolve challenges is not only because of what he or she knows but because of how he or she puts his or her ideas together.

10 | Extending Our Cognitive Resources for Creativity

> Living creatively is really important to maintain throughout your life. And living creatively doesn't mean only artistic creativity, although that's part of it. It means being yourself, not just complying with the wishes of other people.
>
> —Matt Groening

Long-Term Choices to Be More Creative

While we can consciously use our skills to be more creative, it's also important to include in our everyday lives a wider range of experiences and practices that enhance creativity. These can be part of the smallest aspects of our lives, such as keeping a journal for our original ideas, to larger experiences, such as foreign travel or exploratory classes.

Left to our own devices, we tend to select easy, uncreative ideas early in solving most problems. Unless we consciously reach further for ideas, we do the same thing as we have done before, whether it's restaurant choices, conceptual ideas, driving routes, or professional work. We are habitual, and we make choices that are our regular choices. Most people do not seek different or divergent possibilities (Osborn, 1963; Goldschmidt & Tatsa, 2005; Kudrowitz & Wallace, 2013).

In order to counteract our habit for familiarity, it's important to make longer-term, systemic changes to encourage our personal creativity. These are not ones that are major shifts in your life, like moving to a creativity commune, but small changes in your everyday behavior tht can help build a creative lifestyle.

Most cognitive research recognizes that divergent thinking, the basic aspect of creativity, is fueled by connections between ideas and processes in our own brain. These elements are reused, applied differently, and combined to form new results, often without conscious searching or selection. This is because our sub-conscious brain is always active in the generation of creative ideas (Martindale, 1999; Mednick, 1962; Epstein, 1996).

We build our own cognitive raw material through our personal experiences. Having a wider range of cognitive material with which to work logically leads to a broader range of new ideas (Finke, 1992; Epstein, 1996). Without these resources, we are less prone to develop new ideas and more focused on the details of everyday life, whether it's traffic or running our local nuclear reactor.

The unconscious part of our brain has access to all our memories and experiences, which are often hidden from our busy consciousness. While at work, we might not be consciously thinking about our visit to Japan when we were a teenager, but it's still there, deep in our memories, and those experiences might help us solve the problems of today. While we can't go back to our 19-year-old self to encourage ourselves to take such a trip, we can start with increasing the range of experiences we have now.

Having divergent experiences, learning different things, finding different challenges all encourage new and original ideas and thinking. I've seen this in my own research, with first-year college students improving their originality because of the broadening experience of college. After being exposed to a wide range of choices and ideas in their beginning months of college, students can come up with more unusual and therefore original ideas.

The important theory that identifies these positive habits is called Generativity Theory, which was developed by Robert Epstein. His background is in behaviorism, having worked with the renowned psychologist B. F. Skinner. He argues that people's creative output is affected by ongoing personal choices. The areas that can are addressed to help you be more creative include preserving new ideas, seeking challenges, broadening skills and knowledge, and changing physical and social environment.

Recording Ideas

Recording our ideas is perhaps the simplest way to increase and improve our ideas. Part of the challenge of coming up with a new idea comes from the different "schedules" of our brains.

A lot of the time, when we're under pressure to be creative, we can't come up with a new idea for love or money. Our rational and mature brain, in charge most of the time, judges and sorts our ideas, repressing and rejecting the unusual or embarrassing ideas, and advancing the pre-accepted, well-used, less-original ideas. We are constrained by social structure and our own habits, even if we're told to "be creative."

Access to the sub-conscious brain or to our restrained thoughts generally doesn't occur on a regular basis. Our divergent and different ideas seldom slip out of our non-conscious brain into our controlled consciousness, but it does happen when near sleep, when in the shower, when we're relaxed. These are times while our unconscious brain is more able make us aware of unusual combinations. It can also happen if we've practiced being open to more unusual ideas (Martindale, 1999). And perhaps the simplest way to retain these creative ideas and to be more innovative is by recording the ideas that occur at all times.

Ideas newly thought are very ephemeral and very fragile, and recording them quickly is most important. Keeping a journal or notebook by the bed at night will help record those ideas. Having a capability for saving your ideas at any time is what is essential and well recognized in the literature (Epstein, 1996; Lehrer, 2012). The important thing is to have a way to record our ideas everywhere we are. What are some ways you can consistently record your own ideas? Would a notebook, voice recorder, index cards, or a whiteboard next to your bed work better?

Saving the ideas we've had at our leisure can also provide us with the mental resources to solve later problems. The important thing is to move those ideas from easily forgotten to collected, stable resources.

Seeking Challenges

Research holds that we solve problems by working through our previous successful experiences with similar problems and applying those solution types first, only developing new versions as needed. When confronted with a *new* problem, we consciously and subconsciously go through our solution repertoire for similar problems. Unfortunately, that limits our seeking different choices.

We need to seek out challenges to stretch our own capability, to find what's new, and to understand what could happen. Challenges help us develop our ability to tolerate risk and to generate new ideas. The failure that comes with challenge is important to allow people to reasonably weigh risk.

We can see examples of the use of challenges to improve skill in sports. This is a broadly used method in developing athletes. For example, women athletes often practice against male athletes who may be stronger, larger, and/or more highly skilled to increase their own capability (Giles, 2015). We should be doing the same thing with our abilities and experiences, seeking challenges to improve our skills and developing our ability to tolerate risk. Increasing the challenges you attempt will have long-term benefits in spite of the immediate increase in short-term effort.

While it's a good idea to go beyond safe solutions, it's also important to recognize that with every new problem and challenge, there is a high possibly for failure. Results aren't always what we anticipated.

Most experts in the field of creativity and in areas such as design, innovation, or science recognize the value of building from our failures and our experiences (Epstein, 1996). Failures serve to generate more divergent ideas and still provide us with guidelines for positive solutions.

Failure has a bad connotation and is actively avoided in business, government, and education. This prejudice does not encourage experimentation or risk, aspects that could lead to greater creative rewards. Re-labeling these new efforts as "challenges" or "experiments" can enable greater support for trying something innovative and could also be a positive way of looking for more divergent results. We all try to prepare to make our efforts successful, but, if the challenge is substantial, not every new idea is going to work well. But every experiment can offer new understanding.

Change Your Environment

Another way we can grow our creative capabilities is by changing or broadening our social and physical environment on a regular basis. Changing your personal environment is a valuable aspect of building your creativity. It might be as simple as having a range of screen saver images on your computer, different art in your room, or traveling to different cities.

A regular divergent experience is most important, and setting up some habits for diversion can be helpful. Having your computer automatically change the screen saver could work as would having a ritual of changing the desktop background image every Monday morning. Setting up a monthly museum visit or second-hand store exploration could also add to your experiences. And changing your regular commuting route could lead to a range of new discoveries. New experiences also help us develop a tolerance for ambiguity and therefore an openness to new ideas.

We should be conscious of the need to change our environment and our social lives; getting into the habit of seeking new social encounters is a valuable one, whether through work, hobbies, sports, or school. Going off to college is a great way to do this and necessarily changes both your friends and your physical context. At the same time, moving beyond the set of people that we've met at college can also add to the potential for creativity. Similarly, cities, by their density, juxtapose different and interesting ideas and encourage more interaction between divergent groups of people (Johnson, 2010). Travel or work abroad can also build acceptance of a broader range of ideas and a tolerance for ambiguity.

Research has shown that multicultural experiences help to change routine knowledge structures, encourage multiple interpretations of phenomena, and support synthesis of divergent ideas (Leung, et al., 2008).

Broadening Skills and Knowledge

Many times, to be creative requires some level of skill and understanding in a specific area or subject. Learning information and skills in a different subject area will affect your understanding and ideas in your main area of understanding. For example, developed skill in the arts, from music to painting to acting, supports work in other fields such as the sciences. Such talents are more common among Nobel Prize winning scientists than among similarly successful scientists (Grant, 2016). For example, learning to dance Argentine Tango could change your understanding of music, gender roles, or even education (as it did for me). "The more diverse the repertoires of behavior, the more interesting, frequent, and surprising the interconnection" (ibid.). What divergent skills do you wish you had, and which could you develop? These skills might be cooking, music, or bird identification, but all could provide you with cognitive diversity in your life.

The larger challenges of this book have been designed to broaden skills, to be challenging, and to expose learners to other social and physical environments. They are experiences to remember, and that we can continue. All aspects, from recording our ideas to accepting new challenges in work or social life, are ways to develop creativity over the long run that will bear fruit.

Building a Habit to Vary

As we've seen in our own lives, habits are a powerful mental and behavioral tool.

We often do things in an automatic way, having chosen, settled on, or adopted one model, one process, rule, or guideline. This eliminates the need to think and make decisions, whether it's about brushing teeth, vacuuming the floor, or driving the car. We do certain things every day and every week by rote; they are habits. Habits help ensure regular positive results as well as unhealthy or unproductive actions. They are mental short cuts, decided at one time or unconsciously developed over time. While they are routine, they are cognitively valuable as a short cut that saves precious mental energy. They short circuit the need for cognitive efforts such as planning, decisions, or attention.

As repetitive, automatic responses to stimuli or triggers, habits may be the antithesis of creativity; they are doing the same things under the same conditions. With creativity defined as something new and useful, most habits provide, at best, something that is useful, but not always new. We seldom develop habits to make us think about our choices, diversify our responses, or build our creative experience. We need to change that orientation and have a habit that seeks the new and the different. That is the main idea of this book: If you have an ongoing habit of trying new things and seeking new experiences, solving things in a new way, you will become more creative.

Usually, when we address our habits, we try to stop the ones that are bad or negative. Smoking might be a big target, but other dietary and consumption patterns can be equally damaging. Breaking a habit is difficult as the triggers that restart the habit will continue, like having a cookie every time you have a cup of coffee. The real bad habit we have in terms of creativity is one of doing the same old thing.

"If habit and convention are the killers of creativity, then it's the unfamiliar that gives birth to great ideas and innovations" (Kaufman & Gregoire, 2015). Ironically, habits can also help us be more creative, but we need to build a habit for the unfamiliar, the unusual, and the different, a habit of change that will build our skills in creativity. Looking at habits can help us better understand how they work and what we can do to build a habit to change our thoughts, our minds, and our ideas. Extending that idea, we also must accept the idea of constantly seeking the new and the original.

Trying to start a new, positive habit, like exercising or being on time, can be as difficult as stopping a bad habit. The mental effort needed to change habits . . . or to build a new one is substantial (Kahneman, 2011). It's a common saying that starting a new habit requires at least three weeks of constant, mindful change. The time needed to build a habit varies, but recent research indicates an average of 66 days is needed to develop a new habit (Lally, et al., 2010). Developing a new habit requires constant thinking about our choices and making decisions.

As with changes in traits such as developing patience or driving carefully, abstract habits such as creativity are even more challenging to develop or support. Changing the way you think is not directly visible, unlike, for example, dieting. If we go off our diet, we can see the results on a scale, but there's no light that comes on when you're being impatient. And when you're just doing the same old thing, no alarm goes off.

There are some simple, regular habits that can also work to develop, demonstrate, and increase creativity. These include the consistent development of multiple divergent ideas, regularly providing more responses than are required, involving oneself in challenging and different activities, and consistently seeking to be more creative.

Perhaps the most important habit for learners to develop is the **habit to vary**, one of habitually doing divergent things, taking on new challenges as a matter of course, and extending one's limits. It's ironic, a contradiction in terms, as habits are by definition, the same, while change or variance is something that's *not* the same. We can vary many things in our lives, from the routes we travel, to our music choices, to what to have for dinner. Consciously making those changes can have positive effects on our creativity.

The large assignments of the book, the differents, are designed to challenge your habits—to encourage you to move past your current habits of what to eat, how to sleep, and what to wear, but also to develop a larger habit of adventure and exploration. This takes time and repeated practice, and, of course, it requires doing something different.

The overall goal is to recognize when you are making the same choices as you have always made and to consciously make a different choice. For example, we often vary the restaurants we visit, but we frequently have the same prepared dish at each individual restaurant. We generally don't try things we don't like, and we keep ordering the things we *do* like. With the rest of our lives, we've codified our choices as well. This type of socks, that kind of shoes, or this type of shirts all meet the criteria for selection. For example, I buy shirts that are cotton with a button-down collar and are generally in dark colors. Comments from others fly when I wear a white shirt, as breaking my ordinary shirt habit is visible to others.

Any new choice, any "innovation," must be better to replace an existing favorite, and we may not find the new and different to be better. One thing we know will happen is that we may be disappointed in some of the new choices we have made. Short-term failure is a constant aspect in creativity and in design. In order to try something new, in order to innovate, we must leave the status quo, and our new choice might not be a success. (Rogers, 1995) The alternative meal choice at our favorite restaurant might be bland or taste awful. We've tried something new, but the trial run was unsuccessful. Or, of course, the new choice might be our new favorite. But, at the least, we have succeeded at making a divergent choice, one that is not the same done out of habit.

The idea of this process of developing your own creativity is based on your active participation in the learning. You are adding inventive tasks and challenges in your own life. You're also consciously doing them over an extended period of time, which can help you make seeking variety, challenge, and invention a regular part of your life.

Actively doing these creative exercises reinforces your ability and tendency for creativity. Just imagining doing the exercises will not be as effective, just like really winning the lottery is a lot different than *imagining* winning the lottery. This is called "active learning," and it is much more effective than merely listening or reading, or "passive learning." If you actually complete your idea by eating differently, by choosing different routes to and from work, or by switching from a bow tie to a regular straight tie, you will be more affected by your actions and you will be capable of more creative acts. Both this book and my course have been built on the concept of learning by personally doing something. And educational research has found that people who actively complete a task retain much more from the experience than those who only abstractly view or hear about the same task. (See, for example, Marsick, et al., 1999; Prince, 2004; Freeman, et al., 2014.)

Your friends, colleagues, family, and peers all can take an interest and support your development as a creative person. While initially they may see the exercises as silly, they will notice the changes in your creativity. And involving them in the process, in the exploration of new ways of doing things, will be fun for them as well: "Cultivating a spirit of everyday nonconformity can foster the development of personality traits and thinking habits that are important to creative achievement" (Kaufman & Gregoire, 2015).

Do Something Different

One habit most adults share is our daily journey to work or school. We habitually drive the same way home every day. Or we take the same walking route, or connect with transit in the exact same manner. Constrained by bus schedules and car-pools, we might even be on a fixed time schedule.

Our commute to and from work is usually focused on function. Changing it involves fighting the urge for efficiency and saving just a few seconds of precious time, which are often spend doing nothing in particular. Let's imagine taking a slightly different route home from work. The added cost in money or time would be negligible. It could be one block out of the way, or ten blocks out of the way, but the variety of what could be observed and experienced will be worth it.

Here's an example of how we can change one of our regular habits: each day for a week take a different route home from work or school. The second week, add a brief stop, someplace along the way, for a cup of coffee, a newspaper, or to throw trash out of the car. The goal is to break the singular mindset of the commute, to experience different things, even if they really aren't that much different. The change you may experience in your personality could be different as well; stopping someplace for a minute, going into the park you pass, or around a lake, could change your attitude.

Chronicle your routes, experiences, and new things you have discovered. Document your experience in writing and with photographic means.

Building Your Creativity on an Ongoing Basis

A lot of the learning from this book is built on the idea of developing habits: the habit of coming up with a lot of new ideas, the habit of stretching one's capabilities, and, largely, the habit of trying something else. Many of the exercises in the book are relatively short and compact, but attempting all the different challenges will help you build your courage as well as a habit of the divergent and different.

Imagine the habits as our own attributes and that each can be changed. Like with changing the attributes of a refrigerator, some of the habits will be surface features while others might be more substantial or conceptual. For example, I might decide to stop at different places for coffee in the morning, which could either be a minor change in my life or be more substantial if I don't drink coffee in the first place.

As we near the end of this book, we probably understand developing our creativity must be an ongoing process. In order to be creative, we must continually seek to be *more* creative. We can get better at creativity, but becoming more creative is a long-term quest and one with great rewards. The adoption of divergent and original ideas is one of choice and freedom, choosing to try different answers, and freedom from the same old ideas.

And this has to come back to habits. How do we get into the creative habit, the habit to vary? What everyday habits should we accept and nurture to make us more creative? These may include the habits of:

- going past the first answer
- accepting a wider range of possibilities
- working from a wider range of choices
- being courageous in choosing non-familiar solutions
- elaborating and improving our answers
- collaborating with others to generate more ideas, improve ideas, and disseminate ideas, and
- regularly saving ideas we have for another time.

Your Creativity Plan

Developing a plan includes the larger goal, that of becoming more creative. It also includes actions and strategies to reach that goal. As the leading goal is to become creative, there should be strategies and actions that can be continued and that build the **habit to vary** in your everyday life. Actions are specific things you can do, and strategies are groups of ways to meet the larger goal. Strategies would be focusing on divergent thinking and experiences, building social or collaborative support, and reorienting work habits.

Most of the techniques for being more creative are relatively simple; they include generating more ideas, developing habits of trying new and different things, and increasing your own abilities to be adventuresome. At the end of an effort for creativity, however, it's important to have a plan for including these lessons in our regular lives. If we seek to be more creative, and if we do things that help us become more creative, it will have results; now let's develop our own plan.

In developing a plan, questions that could be asked include: What are things I could start today, one thing, so it doesn't get overwhelming? Who could I tell about my effort to be more creative? With whom could I share my creative efforts? Whom could I connect with as a creative partner, and do something different together? How does this extend out to my work or school life?

How do you build a plan for your own creative development? You'll need some scheduled due dates and a way to check back on what you've done. Having some support for your efforts is helpful, someone to report on your effort.

You may also need to develop your own set of rules or goals for varying your behavior and learning from doing something different. That might include never eating the same thing at a restaurant that you had the last time, or eating the same food for dinner, by choice, for one week.

While trying to be creative every day is important, some actions can be done each day, each week, and each month. It will vary with the scope of the changes you are attempting. You need to set your own actions and chart your own progress. Develop a plan with steps to build creativity and other skills that includes methods to increase your involvement with new experiences and people and that has ways for you to seek and find challenges in your life. Here are some questions to guide the development of your plan for building your creativity.

Exercise 10.1: Building a Short-Term Plan

There are some **general** aspects that should be included, such as finding people with whom to share your efforts and who encourage you to continue your development. With whom can you share ideas at work or school? Who is open to new and novel ideas among your friends? Telling a friend of your efforts is a good idea. Note them here:

Names:_____

Names:_____

Each day we can do some things to improve our creativity. Specifically building in a **daily** exercise of your creative capability is a good way to proceed. You should find something you could do each day to be a little different. What will you do each day to improve your creativity?

1. _____

2. _____

3. _____

These could include riding the elevator to a different floor, driving a different route home from work, buying jicama at the grocery store, eating lunch backward, sleeping with just one sock on your foot. Or even wearing something that's just a little different from the norm. Or practicing your ability to generate multiple ideas, or using the "yes, and . . ." method in conversation, or redefining a task.

Weekly: One-time-a-week habits are more planned and can be larger scale. You could schedule time for thinking and daydreaming, talking with a colleague about possible projects, beginning a class on tango, or meeting someone new in a social context.

What are three things you could do once a week that build your capability for creativity? What day and time will you do these in the coming week?

1. _____

2. _____

3. _____

Monthly events are more irregular and can be more ambitious. It would be helpful to have a partner or colleague with whom to collaborate on a regular basis. Things that could be done are going shopping with someone or going to a craft store, a hardware store, a junk shop, or a toy store seeking inspiration and diversion. Designers at the renowned firm IDEO make habit of visiting hardware stores, airplane junkyards, and the Barbie Hall of Fame to spur their ideas (Sawyer, 2008). A monthly goal could also include finding a new colleague with whom to collaborate once a month. You could also attempt a different DSD once a month, and a list of additional Do Something Differents is included in the "Resources" chapter.

List your three ideas here:

1. _____

2. _____

3. _____

11 | **Your Progress**

Creativity takes courage.

—Henri Matisse

As we did at the beginning the book, we'll close the learning experience by looking for change in your use and understanding of creativity. We'll again go through a series of short tests ranging from a self-reported set of observations about your creativity to the Alternative Uses Test and the Remote Associates Test. With each of these, you'll be able to compare your score with your previous effort. What counts here is improvement and change.

As we saw at the beginning of the book, this will give you a good measurement of how much you've developed. The good thing about creativity testing is that you can have fun developing ideas as part of the evaluation, and even the test itself will help you develop your own creativity even more. And the tests will also serve to remind you of ways to improve your creativity. As before, each will take five or ten minutes and will give you an understanding of your creative ability. They're all designed for self-grading.

Exercise 11.1: Your Creativity Survey

Let's begin by reflecting and re-examining our own lives of how creative we are, and the aspects of our lives we could observe that would indicate our capacity for creative behavior. In this exercise is a series of questions; be honest in evaluating yourself as this will help you get an accurate understanding of how creative you are. Once you're done, go back and compare your score with your previous effort.

Exercise 11.1 Your Creativity Survey

Please circle the answer that best describes you and how you are creative.

Circle number: 1 Never 2 Not so much 3 Sometimes 4 Often 5 Most of the time

	Circle number				
	Almost never				Most of the time
1. I think logically to find an answer for problems	1	2	3	4	5
2. I'm good at combining different ideas	1	2	3	4	5
3. I can come up with solutions and ideas most people don't have	1	2	3	4	5
4. I often combine different ideas to solve problems	1	2	3	4	5
5. I am efficient in developing a workable idea	1	2	3	4	5
6. I can come up with more ideas than my friends	1	2	3	4	5
7. My ideas and answers have a lot of detail	1	2	3	4	5
8. Many of my ideas are unusual and eccentric	1	2	3	4	5
9. I'm willing to experiment and try out my ideas in public	1	2	3	4	5
10. I look for different ways to understand a problem	1	2	3	4	5
11. On complex problems, I carefully weigh my choice of a solution	1	2	3	4	5
12. People ask me for ideas when they're stumped	1	2	3	4	5
13. I like to share my solutions and ideas with others	1	2	3	4	5
14. I help other people improve and build on their ideas	1	2	3	4	5
15. I have a lot of different and unusual ideas	1	2	3	4	5
16. I usually find a larger theme in solving any challenge	1	2	3	4	5
17. People seek me out for my unique ideas	1	2	3	4	5

Exercise 11.1 Continued

	Circle number				
	Almost never			Most of the time	
18. People expect me to come up with unusual ideas	1	2	3	4	5
19. I see a number of different solutions in most problems	1	2	3	4	5
20. I work hard to find my best idea quickly as it's more effective	1	2	3	4	5
Total					

Alternative Uses Test

You'll recall that the Alternative Uses Test measures your capability to develop a lot of ideas. This will check on your ability for divergent thinking and reveal progress you have made since the beginning of the book.

This test names a common object and challenges you to develop as many possible alternative uses for the object. To do the test, you'll need a timer, something to write with, and paper to record your ideas. Come up with as many ideas as you can, using the entire time for the challenge. The more answers, the better, even if the ideas are offbeat or strange. See if you can generate more ideas than you did the first time you took the test.

Use the language you use every day to evaluate your creativity with this test.

Imagine you could use as many as you wanted, and that you were not limited to just one size or type of object. Try to think about the most unusual and different uses you can imagine. There are no wrong answers. It's good to be different.

The challenge is to write down as many different and unusual things you can do with a rubber band. Use as many rubber bands as you want, and they can be of any size large or small. Write down your ideas in Exercise 11.2. Start a timer, and you can begin! Make sure you use a full five minutes.

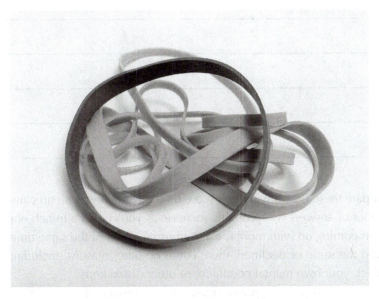

Figure 11.1 Alternative Uses Test: Rubber Band

Exercise 11.2: Alternative Uses Test

1. _____

2. _____

3. _____

4. _____

5. _____

6. _____

7. _____

8. _____

9. _____

10. _____

11. _____

12. _____

13. _____

14. _____

15. _____

Compare these results with your score on the earlier test with tin cans. The number of answers will probably increase as you've had a bunch of practice in coming up with more fun and unusual ideas. At the same time, if it stayed the same or declined, there could be other reasons, including the subject, your own mental condition, or other distractions.

At the end of five minutes, count up your answers. This is your *fluency* score, and it refers to the ability to develop a number of answers to a given challenge.

The second measurement of this test looks at *originality*, the uniqueness or rarity of your answers. Here are the top answers for uses for the image and term "rubber bands": arm band, bracelet, hold hair, bag tie, hold papers, sling shot, make chain, make ball, earring, shoot at someone, and fix something. (These most common answers were gathered from my own online research sources.)

As we know, to be more creative, we're seeking uncommon, unique, and novel answers, so we're looking for answers other than those listed above. Count the number of answers that are still applicable and not on this list of common answers.

Write down the number of ideas you had and note the number of "original" answers you had that weren't on the list of common answers.

Total Answers: _____ Number of Original Answers: _____

Compare this with your first tally.

Thinking of alternative uses for any everyday object is a simple but great task to continue to develop your creativity; it can be done anywhere with any type of object as we've seen in the Toothbrushing Exercise.

Different Consequences

We also need to again test our imagination in addressing real-world problems. It's a more challenging problem, but one that is applicable in measuring our creative capability. Again, an unusual starting point is given to encourage more diverse thinking.

Again, we'll set a timer for five minutes and write down answers to the situation. Here's the challenge:

> Let's imagine you were traveling by air, and, at the midway stop of your flight, there was a long delay between segments of your trip. You're in a large airport; what could you do during a six-hour layover? What are the advantages of this unexpected delay in your schedule? Use the entire five minutes to generate as many possible benefits from this change as possible. Don't limit your answers to those that are obvious or direct, and record as many possible answers as you can.

Once you've used the entire five minutes coming up with possible advantages to the situation, spend five more minutes and add details to each of your answers, on or below the same line; the more, the better. You might also find you have more starting answers as well. This will give a demonstration of your skill for *elaboration*, one of the other ways that creativity is measured.

Exercise 11.3: Consequences Test

1. _____

2. _____

3. _____

4. _____

5. _____

6. _____

7. _____

8. _____

9. _____

10. _____

11. _____

12. _____

13. _____

14. _____

Ideas: _____ Added Details: _____

At the end of the time, count your initial answers to measure your fluency. And then, separately, count the details that were added on each of your answers.

Ideas: _____ Number of Details: _____

You may recall the need for balancing a large number of answers with sufficient details to elaborate each idea. As time is limited, this impacts scores; in the real world, you will usually have more time. Of course, you'll be balancing *fluency* (the number of answers) with *elaboration* (adding the details that explain your answers because of the short time frame).

Remote Associates Test

Making connections is an important aspect of creativity. These connections might be external, with other people, or in our own minds based on our own knowledge and experiences.

One way to test your connection capability is through the Remote Associates Test. You may come up with answers that are different from those given. This is a good indicator of being very creative, going past the expected answer and finding another that is equally correct.

As before, three words will be presented and a fourth, corresponding word will be sought. Give yourself ten minutes for the test. There are 15 elements of varying difficulty. To keep this a reasonable challenge, if it takes more than ten minutes, stop and just record the number completed. Don't, however, work longer than ten minutes unless you like the challenge.

Exercise 11.4: Remote Associates Test

Find the fourth word that fits with the other three in some way, on the front or the back; complete as many as you can in ten minutes. If you finish early, write down your time.

cracker • fly • fighter   _____

cane • daddy • plum   _____

fish • mine • rush   _____

measure • worm • video   _____

sense • courtesy • place   _____

piece • mind • dating   _____

river • note • account   _____

pie • luck • belly   _____

opera • hand • dish   _____

fur • rack • tail   _____

hound • pressure • shot   _____

sleeping • bean • trash   _____

light • birthday • stick   _____

shine • beam • struck   _____

water • mine • shaker   _____

basket • eight • snow   _____

right • cat • carbon _____

nuclear • feud • album _____

cross • rain • tie _____

French • car • shoe _____

Please Record Your Time: _____ Number Completed: _____

Answers/Evaluation of Remote Associates Test

The main way to evaluate the test is by timing the completion of all answers in the allotted time. The word combinations themselves vary in difficulty based on our ordinary use of language.

Again, the capability to answer this test will also vary with English-language ability and context. While the answers below provide an answer, there may be other words that complete the group in ways that are unique to your context.

Answers

cracker • fly • fighter	fire
cane • daddy • plum	sugar
fish • mine • rush	gold
measure • worm • video	tape
sense • courtesy • place	common
piece • mind • dating	game
river • note • account	bank
pie • luck • belly	pot
opera • hand • dish	soap
fur • rack • tail	coat
hound • pressure • shot	blood
sleeping • bean • trash	bag

light • birthday • stick	candle
shine • beam • struck	moon
water • mine • shaker	salt
basket • eight • snow	ball
right • cat • carbon	copy
nuclear • feud • album	family
cross • rain • tie	bow
French • car • shoe	horn

All of these tests can be repeated later in your quest for being more creative. Not only have you become more creative, but you've also learned *how* to become more creative. The main direction of the book has been to help people develop a more divergent set of answers or ideas, from which to choose more appropriate or at least different responses.

Concluding

Througout the book, you have been given a number of challenges that are designed to cultivate creative mental habits. You did things you probably have never done before and things you have only wished you could do.

The work you've done in going through this book is yours, based on your effort in becoming more creative. That effort is something that can continue as you become more creative. While much of the book focused on challenges and exercises, there is also supporting informational material to help you better understand creativity included in the "Resources" chapter, including other books, online resources, and additional Do Something Differents.

This book is founded on a rich body of knowledge on creativity that can support your developing creativity. Your skill has increased, you know more about creativity, and, hopefully, you've had fun becoming more creative.

12 Ten Guides to Being More Creative

In order to attain the impossible, one must attempt the absurd.

—Miguel de Cervantes

One thing that comes up repeatedly when I do workshops and classes on creativity is to find some way to summarize the materials into an easy to remember set of guidelines. Here's my top-ten list on being more creative. And in case of reading ahead, thanks for skipping down to this part to see how the book ends.

The first thing that is important is **your own belief and commitment to becoming more creative**. Everyone is creative, and recognizing your own creativity helps you be more creative. Research by Sternberg (2003) and others shows that people who believe they are creative actually *are* more creative. While they may be honest about their creativity, it could be that the confidence and self-efficacy enable them to develop and put forward more ideas. Even if you believe you are creative, making a conscious and dedicated effort will increase the level of your creativity, as it would with other skills. Value the ideas you generate, and record them in a journal or notebook at any time, as they may have value.

Not only are you creative to begin with, but you can improve how creative you are. **Creativity and intelligence are dynamic and can be increased**. Unfortunately, a lot of people believe that how creative you are or how intelligent you are is set and pre-determined. Neither is fixed at birth, but increasing either takes practice and conscious effort. Recognizing that you can change your abilities, followed by a consistent effort, is productive. Effort at learning both information and skills can pay rewards, and creativity can be increased.

There are other things that can be part of your regular life that indirectly help you be more creative. One should **have an ongoing broad exposure to other ideas** and areas. You should learn to tolerate ambiguity and other ideas. It is important to not judge ideas too quickly, whether they are your ideas or the ideas of others. Instead of rejecting or accepting ideas, examine the value of the ideas, seek to generate ideas to improve them. One way to increase your capability for divergent ideas is to change your physical and social environment. Meeting other people and being exposed to a wide range of different ideas and different environments will help you mix and combine and improve your own thinking. This can occur in many forms: through classes, social events, travel, and new challenges. Research holds that working abroad or in other cultures strongly helps the originality of one's ideas.

The main thing you can actively do is to **develop a habit to vary**. We all need to do things that are different, more challenging, and unusual. As Mae West said: "When caught between two evils, I always like to try the one I've never tried before." If you are always making the unusual choices, whether in what to do or what to eat, you will be exposed to more experiences, and this richness will aid the development of new ideas. If it's a habit, you'll continually reach out for the new. We make a number of choices every day in our lives that are often routine or mindless; make it a habit to try different choices in these incidental aspects of your life. **One critical skill is to find or redefine the problem.** Finding problems to address is an important aspect of creativity. How a problem is defined or conceived often gives direction to how it is solved. One simple way to develop more divergent ideas it to experimentally change the way a problem is described. And at the same time, finding and defining a problem also opens the way to new solutions. We should not be limited in the challenges we address or in the way they are described.

As ideas can be generated without cost and rapidly, **develop multiple answers to any problem**. A good starting number of possible answers is ten. We've seen through research that truly original answers usually aren't the first answers given to any prompt. They are only the most obvious answers. As has been said earlier, the only wrong answer is one answer, and that's because using only one answer does not seek different choices that might be better or transformative. Whenever challenged, provide as many answers as is possible and always more than the number required. Make a conscious effort to develop at least one answer that could be considered wrong or unusual. As Linus Pauling said, "The best way to have a good idea is to have a lot of ideas and then to throw the bad ones away."

We also need to **expand the reach of our ideas by sharing and joining others**. Having good ideas is one thing, but getting those ideas accepted and put to use is an important part of the entire process. Within the field, this is considered innovation, the adoption and dissemination of new and useful ideas; without this part, few ideas will have an impact. At the same time, this means that we need to positively share our ideas with others, whether with individuals or across our organizations. Or even to the public at large.

In order to generate more insights and have a deeper well of inspiration from which to draw, we should **seek challenges for our ideas and persist through obstacles and mistakes and failures**. We do need to be persistent in moving our ideas forward. Not every idea will be accepted by others, and persisting with, adopting, and evolving the ideas will make them better. A good way to develop this persistence is take on challenges where success is not guaranteed. We know that failure is a part of creation; some ideas will succeed, but many won't; being ready for temporary setbacks is an important part of creative problem solving. Recognize that we will need courage to persist in ideas that are new and original; society often seeks the status quo.

We know that not every idea we come up with is good. Therefore, we should be conscious of our thinking and **analyze our ideas and our thinking.** It's very important to think about how we think and how we develop ideas. We need the ability to truthfully evaluate our work and our ideas, comparing them with others and with alternative solutions. We should ask questions about whether our thought process went past our basic assumptions and the most obvious answers.

Contrary to popular conception, instant insight is not available and on demand; creativity does take time and effort, and one should **allow time and purposely daydream**. We should allow time for our ideas to develop and purposely build in time in our schedule to develop new ideas. This means starting early on projects and, at the same time, setting aside thinking time to develop new ideas. It's essential to record our ideas at all times, particularly when we're relaxed and less strict in our evaluation.

Regardless of what we do, internal motivation is the most effective support for creativity. We should **figure out what we love and do it**. Ok, so it's number 11. We all need to find that best part of what we do well and concentrate our efforts in that direction. In most cases, those areas where we have a high level of skill correspond with loving the work. While this doesn't necessarily connect with external reward, this will lead to a more satisfying and positive life. And a more creative life as well.

These points were meant to summarize much of the effort in developing your own creativity; they're not meant to be exhaustive and probably will evolve as time goes on. They're generally based on current research and personal experience with developing creativity.

Resources

www.mycoted.com/Main_Page

This is a site that lists a wide range of creativity techniques.

http://mycreativityskills.com

This site evaluates your lifestyle habits and their effect on your creativity.

https://coggle.it/

Online mindmapping software.

Cited Material

Amabile, T. M. (1998). How to kill creativity (Vol. 87). Boston, MA: Harvard Business School Publishing.

Bronson, P., & Merryman, A. (2010). The creativity crisis. *Newsweek*, July, 12, 2010, p. 44–49.

Castells, M. (2014). *Technopoles of the world: The making of 21st century industrial complexes.* New York: Routledge.

Chaffin, K. (1985). The difference an idea makes: The art of brainstorming. *Activities, Adaptation & Aging, 6*(3), 25–30, DOI: 10.1300/J016v06n03_06

Clinton, G., & Hokanson, B. (2012). Creativity in the training and practice of instructional designers: the Design/Creativity Loops model. Educational Technology Research and Development, 60(1), 111–130.

Cox, G. (2005). *Cox review of creativity in business: Building on the UK's strengths.* HM Treasury. ISBN: 9781845321086.

Coyne, K. P., & Coyne, S. T. (2011). Seven steps to better brainstorming. *McKinsey Quarterly*, 1–6.

Cropley, A. (2006). In praise of convergent thinking. *Creativity Research Journal, 18*(3), 391–404.

Cross, N. (2006). *Designerly ways of knowing* (pp. 1–13). London: Springer.

Csikszentmihalyi, M. (1996). *Flow and the psychology of discovery and invention.* New York: Harper Collins.

Diehl, M., & Stroebe, W. (1987). Productivity loss in brainstorming groups: Toward the solution of a riddle. *Journal of Personality and Social Psychology, 53*(3), 497–509.

Epstein, R. (1996). *Cognition, creativity, and behavior: Selected essays.* Santa Barbara: Praeger Publishers.

Finke, R. A. (1990). *Creative imagery.* Hillsdale, NJ: Lawrence Erlbaumn Associates. Hillsdale, NJ.

Freeman, S., Eddy, S. L., McDonough, M., Smith, M. K., Okoroafor, N., Jordt, H., & Wenderoth, M. P. (2014). Active learning increases student performance in science, engineering, and mathematics. *Proceedings of the National Academy of Sciences, 111*(23), 8410–8415.

Gabora, L. (2002). Cognitive mechanisms underlying the creative process. In T. Hewett and T. Kavanagh (Eds.), *Proceedings of the fourth international conference on creativity and cognition* (pp. 126–133), October 13–16. Lougborough, UK: Loughborough University.

Giles, M. (2015). Retrieved 11.25.16 from https://sports.vice.com/en_us/article/you-will-get-beat-down-the-men-who-practice-with-the-wnba

Goldschmidt, G. (2003). The backtalk of self-generated sketches. *Design Issues, 19*(1), 72–88.

Goldschmidt, G., & Tatsa, D. (2005). How good are good ideas? Correlates of design creativity. *Design Studies, 26*(6), 593–611.

Grant, A. (2016–02–02). *Originals: How non-conformists move the world* (p. 79). New York: Viking.

Grout, D. J. (1973). *A history of western music.* New York: W. W. Norton & Co.

Heilman, K. M., Nadeau, S. E., & Beversdorf, D. O. (2003). Creative innovation: possible brain mechanisms. *Neurocase, 9*(5), 369–379.

Johnson, S. (2010). *Where good ideas come from: The natural history of innovation.* New York: Riverhead Books.

Kahneman, D. (2011). *Thinking, fast and slow.* Danvers, MA: Macmillan.

Kaufman, J. C., & Beghetto, R. A. (2009). Beyond big and little: The four c model of creativity. *Review of General Psychology, 13*(1), 1.

Kaufman, S. B., & Gregoire, C. (2015). *Wired to create: Unraveling the mysteries of the creative mind.* New York: Perigee.

Kim, K. H. (2007). Exploring the interactions between Asian culture (Confucianism) and creativity. *The Journal of Creative Behavior, 41*(1), 28–53.

Kudrowitz, B. K., & Wallace, D. (2013). Assessing the quality of ideas from prolific, early stage product ideation. *Journal of Engineering Design: Special Issue on Design Creativity, 24*(2), 120–139.

Lally, P., Van Jaarsveld, C. H., Potts, H. W., & Wardle, J. (2010). How are habits formed: Modelling habit formation in the real world. *European Journal of Social Psychology, 40*(6), 998–1009.

Land, G., & Jarman, B. (1993). *Breakpoint and beyond: Mastering the future today.* New York: HarperCollins.

Larey, T. S., & Paulus, P. B. (1999). Group preference and convergent tendencies in small groups: A content analysis of group brainstorming performance. *Creativity Research Journal, 12,* 175–184.

Lambert & Dorst, (2009). Design Expertise, New York: Routlege/Architectural Press.

Lehrer, J. (2012). Groupthink: The brainstorming myth. *The New Yorker, 30,* 12.

Leung, A. K. Y., Maddux, W. W., Galinsky, A. D., & Chiu, C. Y. (2008). Multicultural experience enhances creativity: The when and how. *American Psychologist, 63*(3), 169.

Mace, M. A., & Ward, T. (2002). Modeling the creative process: A grounded theory analysis of creativity in the domain of art making. *Creativity Research Journal, 14*(2), 179–192.

Marsick, V. J., & O'Neil, J. (1999). The many faces of action learning. *Management Learning, 30*(2), 159–176.

Martindale, C. (1999). Biological basis of creativity. In R. J. Sternberg (Ed.), *Handbook of creativity* (pp. 137–152). Cambridge, UK: Cambridge University Press.

McMahon, K., Ruggeri, A., Kämmer, J. E., & Katsikopoulos, K. V. (2016). Beyond idea generation: The power of groups in developing ideas. *Creativity Research Journal, 28*(3), 247–257.

Mednick, S. (1962). The associative basis of the creative process. *Psychological Review, 69*(3), 220.

Mink, J. (2000). *Miró*. Cologne: Taschen.

Mottern, R. (2003). Using the rule of six and traditional American Indian learning stories to teach choice theory. *International Journal of Reality Therapy, 23*(1), 27–33.

Osborn, A. F. (1963). *Applied imagination: Principles and procedures of creative problem solving*. New York, NY: Charles Scribners Sons.

Paulus, P. B. (1999). Group creativity. In M. A. Runco and S. R. Pritzker (Eds.), *Encyclopedia of creativity* (pp. 779–784). San Diego: Academic Press.

Petersen, C., & Seligman, M. E. P. (2004). *Character strengths and virtues: A classification and handbook*. New York: Oxford University Press.

Plucker, J. A. (1999). Is the proof in the pudding? Re-analyses of Torrance's (1958 to present) longitudinal data. *Creativity Research Journal, 12*(2), 103–114.

Prince, M. (2004). Does active learning work? A review of the research. *Journal of Engineering Education, 93*(3), 223–231.

Roberts, B. W., O'Donnell, M., & Robins, R. W. (2004). Goal and personality trait development in emerging adulthood. Journal of personality and social psychology, *87*(4), 541–550.

Robinson, K. (2010). Bring on the learning revolution. In *TED talks.*

Rogers, E. (1995). *Diffusion of innovations*, 4th Ed. New York: The Free Press.

Runco, M., & Jaegar, G. (2012). The standard definition of creativity. *Creativity Research Journal, 24*(1), 92–96.

Sawyer, R. K. (2008). *Group genius: The creative power of collaboration*. New York: Basic Books.

Sawyer, R. K. (2011). *Explaining creativity: The science of human innovation*. Oxford: Oxford University Press.

Sawyer, R. K. (2016). How artists create: An empirical study of MFA painting students. *The Journal of Creative Behavior*, DOI: 10.1002/jocb.136

Scott, G., Leritz, L. E., & Mumford, M. D. (2004). The effectiveness of creativity training: A quantitative review. *Creativity Research Journal, 16*(4), 361–388.

Shackleton, J. P., & Sugiyama, K. (1998). Prototype theory and the modelling of new product perception. In B. Jerrard and R. Newport (Eds.), *Managing new product innovation*. Boca Raton: CRC Press.

Simon, H. A. (1978). Rationality as process and as product of thought. *The American Economic Review, 68*(2), 1–16.

Simonton, D. K. (1997). Creative productivity: A predictive and explanatory model of career trajectories and landmarks. *Psychological Review, 104,* 66–89.

Sternberg, R. J. (2003). Creative thinking in the classroom. *Scandinavian Journal of Educational Research, 47*(3), 325–338.

Sternberg, R. J., & Lubart, T. I. (1999). The concept of creativity: Prospects and paradigms. *Handbook of Creativity, 1,* 3–15.

Sutton, R. I. (2002). *Weird ideas that work: 11 1/2 practices for promoting, managing, and sustaining innovation.* New York: Simon and Schuster.

Torrance, E. P. (1968). A longitudinal examination of the fourth grade slump in creativity. *Gifted Child Quarterly, 12,* 195–199.

Underwood Spencer, P. (1990). A Native American worldview. *Noetic Sciences Review, Summer*(15), 14–20.

Van Hoorn, J., Nourot, P., & Alward, K. (1993). *Play at the center of the curriculum.* New York: Macmillan.

Visscher-Voerman, I., & Gustafson, K. L. (2004). Paradigms in the theory and practice of education and training design. *Educational Technology Research and Development, 52*(2), 69–89.

Zhao, Y. (2012). *World class learners* (p. 192). Thousand Oaks, CA: Corwin.

Additional Do Something Differents

Do Something Different: Senses

We all rely on each of our senses to navigate and live in the world, yet many people do not share the full range of senses. They may be blind, deaf, or otherwise limited. For this challenge, limit one of your senses and experience what it is to be without that sense for an extended period of time. This may involve blindfolds or ear plugs, or ways to mute your sense of feeling, but it will give you a different understanding of the world. Record your DSD in writing and by photographs.

Do Something Different: Sleep

Sleeping is a very personal experience, and one that is very routine based. So, for this challenge, sleep differently. Develop three different types of ideas beforehand, and plan your effort. Record your DSD in writing and by photographs.

Do Something Different: Backwards

We all have a set of habits of doing things in certain order. For this challenge, you'll need to do something *backwards* that is out of our expected order. Develop three different types of ideas, and plan your effort. Record your DSD in writing and by photographs.

Do Something Different: With a partner

Invent your own DSD with someone else, completing the DSD physically together. Important to the challenge, your DSD should be inspired by the fact that there are two of you completing the assignment. You may redo one of the other DSDs or create a new one, but *both* of you need to be involved in the same DSD.

Do Something Different

An important part of creativity is convincing others to be more creative. For this DSD, get someone else to do something different. It can be a member of your family or the person that regularly takes your picture for the earlier DSDs, or it could be a complete stranger. Explain to them the nature of the class, and, if they seem interested, ask them for their help. As with other "other" DSDs, you need to allow their creativity to come through and not define exactly what they are to do, and the DSD should not be abusive, illegal, or overly dangerous.

Index